Mum Is Always Right

Words That Celebrate the World's Smartest Mums

Edited and with an Introduction by Patricia Harris

BOOKS

First published in Great Britain in 2009 by
JR Books, 10 Greenland Street, London NW1 OND
www.jrbooks.com

A catalogue record for this book is available from the British Library.

ISBN 978-1-906217-89-1

1 3 5 7 9 10 8 6 4 2

Printed in the UK by CPI Bookmarque, Croydon, CR0 4TD

To my mother,
in her eighty-seventh year.

Contents

Mom Is *Always* Right

Introduction

Mother is a force of nature. She's at least on a par with earth, wind, and fire—and probably more powerful than any of them. As the old Latin proverb reminds us, "Necessity is the mother of invention." Or, as Cervantes observed in *Don Quixote*, "Experience [is] the universal mother of sciences" and "diligence is the mother of good fortune."

When you get right down to it, everything comes from Mum. Every culture throughout recorded time has expressed complete awe at the process of pregnancy, birth, and child-rearing. The flesh-and-blood connection of mother and child is a universal experience, proof of the most loving bond that humans know. It remains an amazing thing that one person produces another. And that power carries immense responsibility.

The myths of Mother loom large in the culture's collective unconscious. The anonymous saying that a "Freudian slip is when you say one thing but mean your mother" reveals a modern American assumption that everything—success or failure, skill or tic—begins with Mum. (How many moms have blurted, in frustration, "That's right—blame your mother!"?)

Mum Is *Always* Right

It could be argued that we live in an age when the convoluted arguments that philosophers once reserved for such pressing matters as how many angels could dance on the head of a pin are now reserved for discussion of all things maternal.

It's no wonder that authors with a poetic sensibility have erected idealized versions of mothers and motherhood. Victorian novelist William Makepeace Thackeray epitomized the sentiment of his day when he wrote, "Mother is the name for God in the lips and hearts of little children."

Far more revealing is the testimony from the trenches of motherhood. Writing with brutal honesty, poet Adrienne Rich captured the mixed emotions of being a mother: "My children cause me the most exquisite suffering of which I have any experience. It is the suffering of ambivalence: the murderous alternation between bitter resentment and raw-edged nerves, and blissful gratification and tenderness." In other words, raising kids can be both exasperating and utterly joyful at the same time.

The sentiment that "all mothers are working mothers" has been so often repeated that the identity of the woman who said it first has been lost. ("Anonymous" is almost invariably female.) Yet, as Golda Meir, former prime minister of Israel, observed, "At work, you think of the children you have left at home. At home, you think of the work you've left unfinished.

Such a struggle is unleashed within yourself. Your heart is rent." Whether a mother spends her weekdays in the office or in the car pool, she has the same goal in mind: raising healthy, happy, secure, and loving children.

The bond of mother and child is universally presumed to be intense at the very least, and all-consuming in the extreme. When the monster Grendel is slain in the *Beowulf* epic, who comes to avenge him? His mother, of course. Only the calamity of orphanhood denies a person the experience of being mothered. We all have an opinion—nay, a whole set of opinions, often contradictory—on the subject.

"To describe my mother would be to write about a hurricane in its perfect power," wrote poet and activist Maya Angelou in awe of the woman who brought her forth. In a similar fashion, comedian Joan Rivers saw her own mother as a force to be reckoned with. "My mother could make anybody feel guilty," Rivers recalled. "She used to get letters of apology from people she didn't even know." The mother's stamp on her daughter, it seems, is indelible. As the prophet Ezekiel wrote, "As is the mother, so is her daughter."

But however verbose daughters can be in their testimony about their mothers, sons have even more to say. Women, perhaps, have the advantage of understanding their mothers as other women. Sons are as mystified by

their mothers as by their wives and daughters. (As American writer Helen Rowland observed, "It takes a woman twenty years to make a man of her son, and another woman twenty minutes to make a fool of him.")

D. H. Lawrence must not have consulted Sigmund Freud when he wrote of his mother, "She is my first, great love." His contemporary, novelist W. Somerset Maugham, was of a different opinion, writing (apparently from experience), "Few misfortunes can befall a boy which bring worse consequences than to have a really affectionate mother." The American sage Ralph Waldo Emerson may have gotten in the first and last word on the mother-son dynamic when he wrote, "Men are what their mothers made them." Yet at heart, every man has the reflexive need to put Mum on a pedestal. (Just get a couple Southern good ol' boys talking about their mamas and you'll swear that every one of their mothers is perched on a cloud with a harp.)

Indeed, only when a woman's child marries does she become a socially sanctioned target of venom and abuse. She then becomes the Mother-in-Law. Even as gentle a soul as Hubert H. Humphrey quipped that "Behind every successful man stands a surprised mother-in-law." Henny Youngman, the comic who made famous the line, "Take my wife—please," regularly explained that he had "just got back from a pleasure trip: I took my mother-in-law to the airport."

The nervous titters at mother-in-law jokes, though, lie in the long comedic tradition of poking fun at the powerful. Those jibes are really just an acknowledgment that the woman was a mother once, and still is. But now she combines the authority of motherhood with the wisdom of experience. Give her a break!

In honor of mums everywhere—sit up straight when you read this book and turn off the TV this instant. You don't want me to have to tell your father, do you?

—*Patricia Harris*

Caretaker of
Future Generations:

Mother

Most of all the other beautiful things in life come by twos and threes by dozens and hundreds. Plenty of roses, stars, sunsets, rainbows, brothers and sisters, aunts and cousins, but only one mother in the whole world.

—Kate Douglas Wiggin

I think a good mother is such a heavenly thing to see. I think it is a gift every bit as beautiful and instinctive as being able to dance across the sky. Maybe I revere it in part. I always have to wonder how I would be.

——Diane Sawyer

A mother's love for her child is like nothing else in the world. It knows no law, no pity, it dares all things and crushes down remorselessly all that stands in its path.

—AGATHA CHRISTIE

What are Raphael's madonnas but the shadow of a mother's love, fixed in a permanent outline forever?

—T. W. Higginson

Mother's love is peace. It need not be acquired, it need not be deserved.

—Erich Fromm

Mother love, particularly in America, is a highly respected and much publicised emotion, and when exacerbated by gin and bourbon it can become extremely formidable.

—Noel Coward

MOTHER'S LOVE GROWS

BY GIVING.

—Charles Lamb

Whatever else is unsure in this stinking dunghill of a world **a mother's love is not.**

—James Joyce

I can't think why mothers love them.
All babies do is leak at both ends.

—Douglas Feaver

A father may turn his back on his child;
brothers and sisters may become inveter-
ate enemies; husbands may desert their
wives and wives their husbands.
But a mother's love endures
through all.

—WASHINGTON IRVING

The only thing a lawyer won't question is the
legitimacy of his mother.
—W. C. Fields

At the heart of mother love

is a desire for the closest thing to immortality that a human being can achieve.

—KATHERINE ELLISON

Women are aristocrats, and it is always the mother who makes us feel that we belong to the better sort.

—John Lancaster Spalding

O wondrous power! How little understood,
Entrusted to the mother's mind alone,
To fashion genius—to form the soul for good.

—Sarah Josepha Hale

According to my method of thinking,
and that of many others, not woman
but the mother is the most precious
possession of the nation, so precious
that society advances its highest well-
being when it protects the functions
of the mother.

—ELLEN KEY

When we see great men and women, we give credit to their mothers. When we see inferior men and women—and that is a common circumstance—no one presumes to the question of the motherhood which has produced them.

— Charlotte Perkins Gilman

So mothers are blamed for their children's problems, on the one hand, or praised for creating healthy, moral citizens on the other, and we may buy into the notion that we're in control of the outcome even when we know better than to believe it.

—Harriet Lerner, PhD

[M]OTHERS GO ON GETTING
BLAMED UNTIL THEY'RE EIGHTY,
BUT SHOULDN'T TAKE IT
PERSONALLY.

—KATHARINE WHITEHORN

It was suddenly discovered that the
mother could be blamed for almost everything. In
every case history of troubled child; alcoholic, sui-
cidal, schizophrenic, psychopathic, neurotic adult;
impotent, homosexual male; frigid, promiscuous
female; ulcerous, asthmatic, and otherwise disturbed
American, could be found a mother.

—Betty Friedan

9

[I]n the current mother mythology, children are seen as eminently perfectible. There are no bad children, only bad parents.

—SHARI L. THURER

BLAMING MOTHER IS JUST A NEGATIVE WAY OF CLINGING TO HER STILL.

—NANCY FRIDAY

The bearing and the training of a child is woman's wisdom.

—*Lord Tennyson*

Who has not watched a mother stroke her child's cheek or kiss her child *in a certain way*, and felt a nervous shudder at the possessive outrage done to a free solitary human soul?

—JOHN COWPER POWYS

Children and mothers never truly part—
Bound in the beating of each other's heart.

—Charlotte Gray

A mother is not a person to lean on
but a person to make leaning unnecessary.
—Dorothy Canfield Fisher

*Everybody knows that a good mother
gives her children a feeling of trust and stability.
She is their earth. She is the one they can count on
for the things that matter most of all.*
—Katharine Butler Hathaway

A mom is a woman whose maternal behavior is motivated by the seeking of emotional recompense for the buffets which life has dealt her own ego. In her relationship with her children, every deed and almost every breath are designed unconsciously but exclusively to absorb her children emotionally and to bind them to her securely.

—Dr. Edward A. Strecker

A woman has two smiles that an angel might envy— the smile that accepts a lover before words are uttered, and the smile that lights on the first born babe, and assures it of a mother's love.

—Thomas C Haliburton

13

Champion Mum

Over her lifetime, a female oyster
may produce more than
100 million young.

The mother-child relationship is paradoxical and, in a sense, tragic. It requires the most intense love on the mother's side, yet this very love must help **the child grow away from the mother and to become fully independent.**

—Erich Fromm

Every mother is like Moses. She does not enter the promised land. She prepares a world she will not see.

—Pope Paul VI

AS A MOTHER I HAVE SERVED LONGER THAN I EXPECTED.

—Carol Emshwiller

God could not be everywhere, and therefore he made mothers.

—Jewish proverb

I have no objection whatsoever to the notion of the
Eternal Father, but every objection to the concept
of an eternal mother.

—Edward VII (attr.)

The real religion of the world comes from women
much more than from men—from mothers most of
all, who carry the key of our souls in their bosoms.
—Oliver Wendell Holmes

If I were damned of body and soul,
I know whose prayers would make me whole,
Mother o' mine, O mother o' mine.

—Rudyard Kipling

GOD IS A MOTHER.

—Eugene O'Neill

*He is Father. Even more, **God is Mother,** who does not want to harm us.*

—*Pope John Paul I*

MOTHERHOOD IS TOO POWERFUL, TOO WEIRD, TOO AWFUL TO BE ANYTHING LESS THAN THE PROVINCE OF GODHOOD.

—JANET MALONEY FRANZE

No one like one's mother
and father ever lived.

—ROBERT LOWELL

Mother is the name for God
in the lips and hearts of little children.
—William Makepeace Thackeray

"Mother" has always been a generic term synonymous with love, devotion, and sacrifice. There's always been something mystical and reverent about them. They're the Walter Cronkites of the human race . . . infallible, virtuous, without flaws, and conceived without original sin, with no room for ambivalence.

—Erma Bombeck

Mother, the Day

The modern observance of Mother's Day began with a campaign launched in 1905 by Anna Jarvis of Philadelphia to honor her own mother, also named Anna Jarvis, who had organized Mothers' Work Days in West Virginia during the Civil War and, after the war, helped reconcile families whose sons had fought on opposing sides. The younger Jarvis suggested white carnations as the official symbol of remembrance on Mother's Day. In 1914 U.S. President Woodrow Wilson declared Mother's Day a national holiday, fixed on the second Sunday in May.

19

Heaven liveth

at the feet of mothers.

—Muhammad

But after God's name, **the name of Mother**
is the sweetest and most holy.
—Samuel Taylor Coleridge

To be a mother is a woman's greatest vocation in life. She is
a partner with God. No being has a position of such power
and influence. She holds in her hands the destiny of nations,
for to her comes the responsibility and opportunity of molding the nation's citizens.

—Spencer W. Kimball

All the earth, though it were full of kind hearts, is but a desolation and a desert place to a mother when her only child is absent.

—Elizabeth Gaskell

She was of the stuff of which great men's mothers are made. She was indispensable to high generation, hated at tea parties, feared in shops, and loved at crises.

—Thomas Hardy

The greatest love is a mother's; then a dog's; then a sweetheart's.

—Polish Proverb

A mother is the truest friend we have, when trials heavy and sudden, fall upon us; when adversity takes the place of prosperity; when friends who rejoice with us in our sunshine desert us; when trouble thickens around us, still will she cling to us, and endeavor by her kind precepts and counsels to dissipate the clouds of darkness, and cause peace to return to our hearts.

—WASHINGTON IRVING

Mother is the dead heart of the family, spending father's earnings on consumer goods to enhance the environment in which he eats, sleeps, and watches television.

—Germaine Greer

The mother cult is something that will set future generations roaring with laughter.

—Gustave Flaubert

AN OUNCE OF MOTHER IS

WORTH A POUND OF CLERGY.

—SPANISH PROVERB

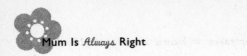

Life was a lot simpler when what we honored was father and mother rather than all major credit cards.
—Robert Orben

A mother is a watchdog, a lioness, an idiot.
So one mustn't reason with her.
—Carl Ewald

So it must needs be a horribly wicked thing ever to forget, or willfully to vex a Father or a Mother, especially a mother.

—Samuel Taylor Coleridge

24

I cannot bear a mother's tears.
—Virgil

Who takes the child by the hand takes the mother by the heart.
—Danish Proverb

A mother's love is patient and forgiving when all others are forsaking, and it never fails or falters, even though the heart is breaking.

—Helen Steiner Rice

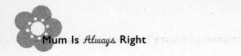

"M" is for the million things she gave me,

"O" means only that she's growing old,

"T" is for the tears she shed to save me,

"H" is for her heart of purest gold;

"E" is for her eyes, with love-light shining,

"R" means right, and right she'll always be,

Put them all together, they spell "MOTHER,"

A word that means the world to me.

—HOWARD E. JOHNSON
(1915 SONG)

A mother is a person who seeing there are only four pieces of pie for five people, promptly announces she never did care for pie.

—Tenneva Jordan

A MOTHER'S ARMS ARE MORE COMFORTING THAN ANYONE ELSE'S.

—DIANA, PRINCESS OF WALES

A mother's arms are made of tenderness, and children sleep soundly in them.

—Victor Hugo

27

THERE'S NOTHING LIKE
A MAMA-HUG.

—ADABELLA RADICI

The sweetest sounds to mortals given
Are heard in Mother, Home,
and Heaven.

—*William Goldsmith Brown*

Youth fades; love droops, the leaves of friendship fall;
A mother's secret hope outlives them all.

—Oliver Wendell Holmes

The heart of a mother is a deep abyss at the bottom of which you will **always find forgiveness.**

—HONORÉ DE BALZAC

The mother's heart is the child's schoolroom.

—Henry Ward Beecher

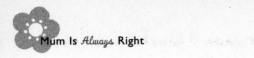

One good mother
is worth a hundred schoolmasters.

—George Herbert

Mother is far too clever to understand
anything she does not like.

—Arnold Bennett

The best academy, **a mother's knee.**

—James Russell Lowell

A FREUDIAN SLIP IS WHEN
YOU SAY ONE THING BUT
MEAN YOUR MOTHER.

—UNKNOWN

You don't have to deserve your mother's love.
You have to deserve your father's.
—Robert Frost

All women dress like their mothers, that is their
tragedy. **No man ever does. That is his**.

—Alan Bennett

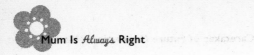

Why is it that in our society women are the primary caretakers? The question has triggered a number of theories among behavioral scientists. But whatever the discipline, all theorists concur on one point:

The emotional tie between a mother and her child is more intense than that between father and child.

—LOUIS GENEVIE, PhD, AND EVA MARGOLIES

I am sure that if the mothers of various nations could meet, there would be no more wars.

—E. M. Forster

A mother's hardest to forgive.
Life is the fruit she longs to hand you,
Ripe on a plate. And while you live,
Relentlessly she understands you.

—Phyllis McGinley

Sadly, the enormity of a mother's job often goes unnoticed—by men, by women who are not mothers, and by society in general. This, we believe, is a dire oversight. Not only are mothers the caretakers of future generations, but models for a more loving, giving existence. To be a mother is to move outside oneself, to give of oneself in a way that is unheralded in the human experience.

—Louis Genevie, PhD, and Eva Margolies

I really learned it all from mothers.

—Dr. Benjamin Spock

The Adventure to End All Adventures:

Motherhood

MOTHERHOOD IS LIKE
ALBANIA—YOU CAN'T TRUST THE
DESCRIPTIONS IN THE BOOKS,
YOU HAVE TO GO THERE.

—MARNI JACKSON

Motherhood is the second oldest profession in the world. It never questions age, height, religious preference, health, political affiliation, citizenship, morality, ethnic background, marital status, economic level, convenience, or previous experience. It's the biggest on-the-job training program in existence.

—Erma Bombeck

I affirm my profound belief that **God's greatest creation is womanhood.** I also believe that there is no greater good in all the world than motherhood. The influence of a mother in the lives of her children is beyond calculation.

—James E. Faust

Motherhood is a wonderful thing—what a pity to waste it on children.

—Judith Pugh

CHILDREN REINVENT
YOUR WORLD FOR YOU.
—SUSAN SARANDON

37

Motherhood is neither a duty nor a privilege, but simply the way that humanity can satisfy the desire for physical immortality and triumph over the fear of death.

—Rebecca West

At age thirty-eight, when I decided that I wanted to have a child, I decided it in the spirit of adventure. Having a child was a trip I didn't want to miss. Of course I had no idea then that motherhood was the adventure to end all adventures.

—Susan Cheever

Motherhood affords an instant identity. First, through wifehood, you are somebody's wife; then you are somebody's mother. Both give not only identity and activity, but status and stardom of a kind.

—Betty Rollin

I love being a mother. . . . I am more aware. I feel things on a deeper level. I have a kind of understanding about my body, about being a woman.

—Shelley Long

39

Motherhood brings as much joy as ever, but it still brings boredom, exhaustion, and sorrow too. Nothing else ever will make you as happy or as sad, as proud or as tired, for nothing is quite as hard as helping a person develop his own individuality especially while you struggle to keep your own.
—Marguerite Kelly and Elia Parsons

MOTHERHOOD HAS A VERY HUMANIZING EFFECT. EVERYTHING GETS REDUCED TO ESSENTIALS.

—Meryl Streep

When you are a mother, you are never really alone in your thoughts. You are connected to your child and to all those who touch your lives. A mother always has to think twice: once of herself and once for her child.

—Sophia Loren

There is nothing more thrilling in this world, I think, than having a child that is yours, and yet is mysteriously a stranger.

—Agatha Christie

You realize after you have had children that you'll never love anything more than your child.

—Kate Hudson

Having three children and watching them influence each other is so beautiful to me. I'm so blessed that's my family. As a mom, I just want more kids—I'm having a great time.

—Angelina Jolie

Surprise!

Researchers for the *Motherhood Report* found that, despite the availability of birth control, only 54 percent of first children, 58 percent of second children, and 34 percent of youngest children were planned.

My point is that no matter what the ordinary person says . . . no matter who it is that speaks, or what superlatives are employed, no baby is admired sufficiently to please the mother.

—E. V. Lucas

THERE'S ONLY ONE PRETTY CHILD IN THE WORLD, AND EVERY MOTHER HAS IT.

—PROVERB

A soiled baby, with a neglected nose, cannot be conscientiously regarded as a thing of **beauty.**

—Mark Twain

Motherhood is the most essential relationship to the continuity of life—and the wiping of snotty noses. It possesses the tenderness of a Mary Cassatt painting one minute, the surreality of a Diane Arbus photo the next.

—Camille Peri and Kate Moses

Motherhood is the strangest thing, it can be like being one's own Trojan horse.

—REBECCA WEST

Over the years I have learned that motherhood is much like an austere religious order, the joining of which obligates one to **relinquish all claims to personal possessions.**

—Nancy Stahl

A mother has, perhaps, the hardest earthly lot; and yet no mother worthy of the name ever gave herself thoroughly for her child who did not feel that, after all, she reaped what she had sown . . .

—Henry Ward Beecher

Motherhood has relaxed me in many ways. You learn to deal with crisis. I've become a juggler, I suppose. It's all a big circus, and nobody who knows me believes I can manage, but sometimes I do.

—JANE SEYMOUR

MOTHERHOOD WAS MY TRIGGER-
ING POINT FOR TRYING TO UN-
DERSTAND THE MEANING OF LIFE.

—MADONNA

FAR FROM DEPRIVING ME OF
THOUGHT, MOTHERHOOD GAVE
ME NEW AND STARTLING THINGS
TO THINK ABOUT AND THE
MOTIVATION TO DO THE HARD
WORK OF THINKING.

—JANE SMILEY

Whatever mix of happiness and sorrow it brings, a commitment to fostering growth expands a mother's intellectual life. . . . [C]hildren are fascinating. Even as caring for children may reawaken a mother's childhood conflicts, in favorable circumstances her children's lively intellects rekindle her own. The work of fostering growth provokes or requires a welcoming response to change.

—SARA RUDDICK

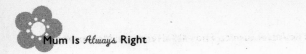

My mother groaned! My father wept. Into the Dangerous world I leapt.

—WILLIAM BLAKE

When you have children, you all of a sudden empathize with your parents more, **you understand what it was like for them to love you.**

—Laura Bush

Something intense, unique, special, serious, and over-whelming naturally occurs between a mother and a child that becomes the focal point of the mother's life. She has created new life in her body—a life totally dependent upon her goodwill and good sense.

—Dr. Laura Schlessinger

As a parent, even of a young child, I often feel the tug of that weight, the easy gravity, that comes with the position. My marriage, my death, my failures or successes, my daily kindnesses or meannesses, all mean more, because they will be felt by a person other than my-self as central, determining.

—Mona Simpson

Having children changes your life irrevocably. It takes the whole paradigm and turns it upside down in the most wonderful way. Until you have a child, you've never been certain you'd give your life for someone, you've never been so proud, you've never been so tired.

—Elizabeth Vargas

I view my role in politics as an extension of my role as a mother and grandmother. The reasons I came to Congress are simple: the children, the children, the children.

—Nancy Pelosi

After [the 1992] election, forty-seven
women went to the House, eight to the
Senate. . . . For the first time it was possible to measure statistically what we knew
instinctively—that women in office make
a difference on key issues. . . . One good
example: gun control. Women see this as
a "mommy issue"—no machine guns on
the playgrounds, good idea! The ban on
assault weapons would have never passed
Congress had there been fewer women
in 1993.

—COKIE ROBERTS

**Maternity is on the face of it an unsocial ex-
perience.** The selfishness that a woman has learned to
stifle or to dissemble where she alone is concerned, blooms
freely and unashamed on behalf of her offspring.

—Emily James Putnam

Oh what a power is motherhood,
possessing a potent spell. All women alike **fight
fiercely for a child.**

—Euripides

*I love motherhood more than anything.
It's like it's the whole reason for my existence now.*

—Kate Winslet

Je Ne Regrette Rien

Although motherhood has its trials, only 4 percent of mothers surveyed reported that they probably or definitely would not become mothers if they had the choice to do it all over again.

The joy of parenthood is to experience the development of a "lively" child into a fine human.

—Ruth Bader Ginsburg

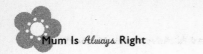

SOMETIMES WHEN I LOOK AT
MY CHILDREN, I SAY TO MYSELF,
"LILLIAN, YOU SHOULD
HAVE STAYED A VIRGIN."

—LILLIAN CARTER

Successful motherhood is a unique
form of responsibility-taking, rooted in an understanding of competing demands, compromise,
nurture, making the best of things, weighing often
competing limitations, in order to arrive at a
realistic mode of survival.

—Jane Smiley

Pride is one of the seven deadly sins; but it cannot be the pride of a mother in her children, for that is a compound of two cardinal virtues—faith and hope.

—Charles Dickens

THERE IS ONLY ONE PRETTY
CHILD IN THE WORLD, AND EVERY
MOTHER HAS IT.

—CHINESE PROVERB

Family life itself, that safest, most traditional, most approved of female choices, is not a sanctuary: it is, perpetually, a dangerous place.

—MARGARET DRABBLE

WHAT A PRICE WE PAY FOR THE GLORY OF MOTHERHOOD.

—ISADORA DUNCAN

[T]he woman is universally sacrificed **to the wife and mother.**

—Elizabeth Cady Stanton

Womanliness means only motherhood;
All love begins and ends there—roams enough,
But, having run the circle, rests at home.

—Robert Browning

56

Women do not have to sacrifice person-hood if they are mothers. They do not have to sacrifice motherhood in order to be persons. Liberation was meant to expand women's opportunities, not to limit them. The self-esteem that has been found in new pursuits can also be found in mothering.

—ELAINE HEFFNER

There is cool water in being a mother, there is steam; there is salt, there is sweetness, there is bitter, there is utterly delicious.

—Anne Lamott

57

I felt that I had learned a great deal about mothers by being one, but that I had become in some way a less objective observer of children.

—Margaret Mead

My own mommy war is internal, waged as a battle against the swift passage of time. My soft toddlers are now sinewy and hard. They steal my Victoria's Secret catalogs and get instant messages that make me more certain than ever that the definition of a good mother is "a woman who spends enough time with her children to know what the hell they are doing."

—Iris Krasnow

The Body's Interior Landscape:

Childbearing

In the sheltered simplicity of the first days after a baby is born, one sees again the magical closed circle, the miraculous sense of two people existing only for each other.

—Anne Morrow Lindbergh

Although they tell you you are most beautiful when you're pregnant, all the models who epitomize beauty have skinny waistlines. So they're shitting you right from the start.

—Florynce Kennedy

60

Although I belong to the lucky generation of the pill, it never occurred to me
that motherhood was optional; I assumed
it with the stern determination of a true
fanatic.

—ISABEL ALLENDE

Making the decision to have a child—it's momen-
tous. It is to decide forever to have **your heart
go walking outside your body.**

—Elizabeth Stone

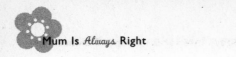

It was a step forward in the passionate journey—and one made possible by it—for educated women to say "yes" to motherhood as a conscious human purpose and not a burden imposed by the flesh.

—BETTY FRIEDAN

The best thing that could happen to motherhood already has. Fewer women are going into it.

—Victoria Billings

BIOLOGY IS THE LEAST OF WHAT MAKES SOMEONE A MOTHER.

—OPRAH WINFREY

Of all the rights of women, the greatest is to be a mother.

—Lin Yutang

I was not a girl carried away by a passion for babies. I didn't avoid them, but neither did they loom large in my ambitions.... In the end I agreed to give it a try because I figured it might be one of those things I'd regret never having done, like eating sushi or riding the Cyclone at Coney Island. ...I was worried that if I didn't do it, I would always **wonder what I'd missed.**

—Amy Herrick

I am serious about wishing I had children, beautiful children. I wouldn't care for the other variety.

—Tallulah Bankhead

Motherhood is never honored by excessive talk about the heroics of pregnancy.

—LEONARD FEENEY

I figured having a baby past forty was no big deal these days. After all, everyone's doing it—if I remember my *People* magazine cover stories correctly—I was just following the trends. And yet you'd think Grandma Moses had walked into this obstetrician's office.

—Susan Konig

Why do pregnant women become nauseous? Because the first time you realize that there's something alive in there . . . you puke.

—MEL BROOKS

Oldest Mum

Satyabhama Mahapatra, a sixty-five-year-old retired schoolteacher in India, became the world's oldest mother when she gave birth to a baby boy on April 9, 2003. Although she and her husband had been married fifty years, it was their first child and was conceived through artificial insemination using eggs from the woman's twenty-six-year-old niece, Veenarani Mahapatra, and the sperm of Veenarani's husband.

In our own beginnings, we are formed
out of the body's interior landscape. For
a short while, our mothers' bodies are the
boundaries and personal geography which
are all that we know of the world.

—Louise Erdrich

Lovers make you a gift of your body;
so do children. The body again becomes
distinct, edged, a marvel you'd forgotten,
retrieved by the unexpected: your belly
slimy with gel, fingers and toes waving
like sea anemones on a grainy sonogram
screen.

—Kate Moses

66

Anyone who thinks women are the weaker sex never witnessed childbirth.

—Unknown

Our birth is but a sleep and a forgetting: The soul that rises with us, our life's star, Hath had elsewhere its setting, And cometh from afar. Not in entire forgetfulness, And not in utter nakedness, But trailing cloud of glory do we come From God, who is our home: Heaven lies about us in our infancy.

—William Wordsworth

67

I'm twenty pounds bigger already, and my feet just swelled up today! Fortunately for me, I'm loving every second of it. What makes you feel beautiful is that you're creating something.

—Kate Hudson, on being pregnant

A ship under sail and a big-bellied woman are the handsomest two things that can be seen common.

—Benjamin Franklin

Getting pregnant doesn't excite me, but having kids does. I know I'll be a mother someday. It's just that . . . I don't really want to look like a whale, you know? But I'm sure the idea of something growing inside you is pretty powerful.

—Charlize Theron

If men could get pregnant,
abortion would be a sacrament.

—FLORYNCE KENNEDY

You've learned that there are three
stages to being pregnant. . . . During
the first trimester, you have morning
sickness; during the second, you buy
overpriced maternity clothes, and
during the third you look radiant (or
at least everyone acts sweet and tells you
that you do) while you waddle and wait.

—AMY EINHORN

If pregnancy were a book,
they would cut the last two chapters.
—Nora Ephron

*Once, miserable and uncomfortable and huge,
I said "screw it," and parked in the handicapped
space nearest the drugstore. One glance at me
heading toward him and the cop tore up the ticket
he'd been writing. Pregnancy was power.*
—Janet Maloney Franze

Overall it's been so easy and happy. I haven't been
weepy or angry, just on this happy high all the time.
I'm a twenty-four-hour giggle box.

—Julia Roberts, on being pregnant with twins

In the pregnancy process I have come to realize how much of the burden is on the female partner. She's got a construction zone going on in her belly.

—AL ROKER

**If men had to have babies,
they would only have one each.**
—Diana, Princess of Wales

I never liked dessert before, but during the pregnancy, it was all about chocolate and whipped cream and cakes.

—EVA HERZIGOVA

By far the most common craving of pregnant women is **not to be pregnant.**

—*Phyllis Diller*

I am not finding pregnancy much of a joy. I am afraid of childbirth, but I am afraid I can't find a way of avoiding it.

—Brigitte Bardot

DEATH AND TAXES AND CHILD-
BIRTH! THERE'S NEVER ANY CON-
VENIENT TIME FOR ANY OF THEM!

—Margaret Mitchell

Unto the woman he said, I will greatly multiply thy sorrow and thy conception; in sorrow thou shalt bring forth children.

—Genesis 3:16

There are six billion birth stories in the world. Good luck finding a woman who will tell you **what hers was really like.**

—Rahna Reiko Rizzuto

If you want to know how childbirth feels, just take your bottom lip and pull it over your head.

—CAROL BURNETT

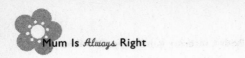

Having a baby is like trying to
push a grand piano through a transom.
—ALICE ROOSEVELT LONGWORTH

I never believed I would *really* become pregnant, because the thought of having an entire person grow
inside your body is such a bizarre idea that only
lunatics or religious fanatics would take for granted
the fact that it might actually happen. And then
there is the matter of getting the baby out, which is
something no normal person wants to think about.
—Harriet Lerner, PhD

After a fairly shitty pregnancy—nine months of ambivalence about a surprise conception at age thirty-nine—I was stunned by how glorious the birth was. I fully expected to be yelling for drugs like Elvis and am glad I didn't. They really need to have different words for pain. Childbirth is more like doing a marathon without moving an inch.

—Sarah Bird

I think that carrying a baby
inside of you is like running
as fast as you can. It feels like
finally letting go and filling
yourself up to the widest limits.

—Unknown

*Holding your firstborn, your wife looks at you
through different eyes, a traveler from another country.
The mothering cues are clearly rooted very deep in the
female psyche.*

—Charlton Heston

The moment a child is born, the mother is also born. She never existed before. The woman existed, but the mother, never. A mother is something absolutely new.

—RAJNEESH

Those of us who give our genes as well as our love to children set out to reproduce . . . ourselves. We deliver unconscious expectations in the birthing room. We think we know them because they are ours.

—Ellen Goodman

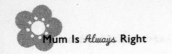

THE MOMENT I HELD HER
IN MY ARMS, I BECAME A DIF-
FERENT PERSON. YOU COULD SAY
THAT I JOINED THE HUMAN RACE.
FOR THE FIRST TIME IN MY LIFE,
MY CONNECTION WITH SOMEONE
ELSE SLICED THROUGH THE WEB
OF DEFENSES, FEAR, AND PRIDE
THAT HAD SEPARATED ME
FROM THE WORLD.

—SUSAN CHEEVER,
ON FIRST HOLDING HER DAUGHTER

I carry from my mother's womb a fanatic's heart.

—William Butler Yeats

People say, when you have children, everything changes. But maybe things are awakened that were already there.

—Meryl Streep

Becoming a mother makes you the mother of all children. From now on each wounded, abandoned, frightened child is yours. You live in the suffering mothers of every race and creed and weep with them. You long to comfort all who are desolate.

—Charlotte Gray

I looked down at him in adoration and then I looked up and saw hanging over our heads, like a grand piano on a piece of dental floss, the mortal nature of all that we are. In a flash, I knew that not only were all my worries not over, they were just beginning.

—Amy Herrick, on first seeing her son

When a child enters the world through you, it alters everything on a psychic, psychological, and purely practical level. You're just not free anymore to do what you want to do. And it's not the same again. Ever.

—Jane Fonda

I wish either my father or my mother, or indeed both of them, as they were in duty equally bound to it, had minded what they were about when they begot me.

—Laurence Sterne

MOTHERS ARE FONDER THAN FATHERS OF THEIR CHIL- DREN BECAUSE THEY ARE MORE CERTAIN THEY ARE THEIR OWN.

—ARISTOTLE

Mothers are a biological necessity;
fathers are a social invention.

—MARGARET MEAD

Biological possibility and desire
are not the same as biological need.
Women have childbearing equipment.
For them to choose not to use the equipment is no more blocking what is instinctive than it is for a man who, muscles or
no, chooses not to be a weightlifter.

—BETTY ROLLIN

The miest

Known to history only as the first wife of Feodor Vassilyev (1707–82) of Shuya, Russia, Mrs. Vassilyev holds the record for the largest officially recorded number of children ever born to one mother: sixty-nine. In twenty-seven confinements between 1725 and 1765, she gave birth to sixteen pairs of twins, seven sets of triplets, and four sets of quadruplets. All but two of her children survived infancy.

Women's liberation is just a lot of foolishness. It's the men who are discriminated against. They can't bear children. And no one's likely to do anything about that.

—Golda Meir

CHILDREN ARE THE ANCHORS THAT HOLD A **MOTHER TO LIFE.**

—SOPHOCLES

84

[My mother] also tells the story of my birth.
I'm almost half kidding when I say, I came out and waved. My mother says that I came out head, arm, other arm, thumb in mouth, immediately. They were astounded, because generally that's not what you do. I was born clear, you know.

—Whoopi Goldberg

To see my dimples in her makes me like my dimples because I share them with her.

—Jennifer Garner, on daughter Violet

You can sort of be married, you can sort of be divorced, you can sort of be living together, **but you can't sort of have a baby.**

—David Shire

It sometimes happens, even in the best of families, that a baby is born. This is not necessarily cause for alarm. The important thing is to keep your wits about you and borrow some money.

—*Elinor Goulding Smith*

Although your baby might weigh upward of eight pounds, chances are you'll have only lost a couple more than that. This will be depressing. So don't get on the scale, and eat those cookies. . . .
[H]aving just *had* a baby is the only time in your life when you can be overweight without apology.

—AMY EINHORN

I like trying [to get pregnant]. I'm not so sure about childbirth.

—GEORGE ELIOT

Mother —that was the bank where we deposited all our hurts and worries.

—T. DeWitt Talmage

With the birth of each child, you lose two novels.

—Candia McWilliam

Many people have said to me, "What a pity you had such a big family to raise. Think of the novels and the short stories and poems you never had time to write because of that." And I looked at my children and I said, "These are my poems. These are my short stories."

—Olga Masters

I have a dream version where I think, maybe in four years I'll have two in a row really quickly again—how fabulous to have a whole bunch of them! But then at that point, when everyone's potty-trained and sleeping through the night, are you really going to go back?

—Gwyneth Paltrow,
on the possibility of having more children

Her dignity consists in being unknown to the world; her glory is in the esteem of her husband; her pleasures in the happiness of her family.

—Jean Rousseau

The most effective form of birth control I know is spending the day with my kids.

—JILL BENSLEY

The mother of the year
should be a sterilized woman
with two adopted children.

—PAUL EHRLICH

Somewhere on this globe, every ten
seconds, there is a woman giving birth to a child.
She must be found and stopped.

—Sam Levenson

No Calling In Sick:

Child-Raising

MOTHER
KNOWS BEST.

—Godey's Lady's Book and Magazine, MAY 1871

It is pretty generally held that all a woman needs to do to know all about children is to have some. This wisdom is attributed to instinct. ... I have seen mothers give beer and spaghetti and Neapolitan ice cream to children in arms, and if they got that from instinct, the only conclusion possible is that instinct is not what it used to be.

—Heywood Broun

The more people have studied different methods of bringing up children, the more they have come to the conclusion that what good mothers and fathers instinctively feel like doing for their babies is the best after all.

—Dr. Benjamin Spock

MATERNAL INSTINCT, MERELY AS AN INSTINCT, IS UNWORTHY OF OUR SUPERSTITIOUS REVERENCE.

—CHARLOTTE PERKINS GILMAN

In the course of a day, I'll find myself going from an interview about the situation in Iraq to a conversation about a colleague's baby's tummy troubles. After a few times of hearing both me and the doctor say things like, "Cheese, bananas, and rice," the young women stop bothering the doctor and just check in with experienced mothers.

—Cokie Roberts

I confess that I'm still not crazy for other children. But I can't explain how the weight of my daughter in my arms calms me, sustains me, and sometimes makes me deliriously happy. I'm not convinced that every woman has a maternal instinct, but that we are all born with the capacity to love and nurture.

—Elissa Schappell

My children cause me the most exquisite suffering of which I have any experience. It is the suffering of ambivalence: the murderous alternation between bitter resentment and raw-edged nerves, and blissful gratification and tenderness.

—Adrienne Rich

If there were no schools to take children away from home part of the time, the insane asylums would be filled with mothers.

—E. W. Howe

95

Priceless

Based on salary data from the U.S. Bureau of Labor Statistics, among other sources, Edelman Financial Services estimates that the median annual salary for the tasks a stay-at-home mother performs should be $773,700.

I feel very blessed to have two wonderful, healthy children who keep me completely grounded, sane, and throw up on my shoes just before I go to an awards show just so I know to keep it real.

—Reese Witherspoon

Sometimes the laughter in mothering is the recognition of the ironies and absurdities. Sometimes, though, it's just pure, unthinking delight.

—BARBARA SCHAPIRO

I will never understand children.

I never pretended to. I meet mothers all the time who make resolutions to themselves. "I'm going to develop patience with my children and go out of my way to show them I am interested in them and what they do. I am going to understand my children." These women wind up making rag rugs using blunt scissors.

—Erma Bombeck

Discipline is a symbol of caring to a child. He needs guidance. If there is love, there is no such thing as being too tough with a child. A parent must also not be afraid to hang himself. If you have never been hated by your child, you have never been a parent.

—Bette Davis

The House Democratic Caucus is blessed by the diversity of its members. Just as I do as a mother, as speaker, I intend to do a great deal of listening. But when necessary, I am not afraid to use my mother-of-five voice to ensure that I am heard.

——Nancy Pelosi

THE HAND THAT
ROCKS THE CRADLE
RULES THE WORLD.

—PROVERB

SPOIL YOUR HUSBAND,
BUT DON'T SPOIL
YOUR CHILDREN—
THAT'S MY PHILOSOPHY.

—LOUISE SEVIER GIDDINGS CURREY,
FTD MOTHER OF THE YEAR, 1961

Tired mothers find that spanking takes less time than reasoning and penetrates sooner to the seat of the memory.

—Will Durant

A mother's feeling that she needs to control her child's behavior is a major source of stress in mothering. . . . We see in our children our own reflection, and when we don't like what we see, we feel angry.

—Elaine Heffner

Experts say you should never hit your children in anger. When is a good time?

When you're feeling festive?

—Roseanne Barr

Some mothers are kissing mothers and some are scolding mothers, but it is love just the same, and most mothers kiss and scold together.

—Pearl S. Buck

Motherhood, in short, is powerful assertiveness training. Even the most timid woman may soon realize that her life will quickly go downhill if she doesn't establish some authority over a recalcitrant toddler.

—Katherine Ellison

One reason I think we get so angry at our children is because we can. Who else can you talk to like this? Can you imagine hissing at your partner, "You get off the phone *now!* No, *not* in five minutes . . ."? Or saying to a friend, "You get over here right this second! And the longer you make me wait, the worse it's going to be for you."

—BETH MYLER

There is nothing like staying at home for real comfort.

—JANE AUSTEN

THE STORY OF A MOTHER'S LIFE: TRAPPED BETWEEN A SCREAM AND A HUG.

—CATHY GUISEWITE

I'm the disciplinarian. Guy's the spoiler. When Daddy gets home, they're going to get chocolate. I'm a more practical person—I worry about their teeth ... what they wear, making sure they're getting their homework done.

—Madonna

Now, any parenting expert will tell you what to do when your two-year-old swears. You ignore it. . . . Because if you react . . . the child will know that something is *very special* about that word, and it will become the Word of Choice.

—SANDI KAHN SHELTON

Don't Talk to Your Mother Like That!

A 1646 Massachusetts law provided that a child over the age of sixteen "who shall curse or smite their natural father or mother . . . shall be put to death."

FATHERS DON'T CURSE,
THEY DISINHERIT.
MOTHERS CURSE.

—IRMA KURTZ

It's not easy being a mother.
If it were easy, fathers would do it.
—Bea Arthur, as Dorothy on The Golden Girls

ONE HOUR WITH A CHILD
IS LIKE A TEN-MILE RUN.
—JOAN BENOIT SAMUELSON,
OLYMPIC GOLD MEDALIST IN THE MARATHON

It's good to remember that our children
are always watching us.
—Laura Bush

Who ran to help me when I fell,
And would some pretty story tell,
Or kiss the place to make it well?
My mother.

—Ann Taylor

True motherhood is the most beautiful of all arts, the greatest of all professions. She who can paint a masterpiece or who can write a book that will influence millions deserves the plaudits and admiration of mankind; but she who rears successfully a family of healthy, beautiful sons and daughters whose immortal souls will be exerting an influence throughout the ages ... deserves the highest honor that man can give.

—David O. McKay

Life was diapers and little jars of pureed apricots and bottles and playpens and rectal thermometers, and all those small dirty faces and all those questions.

—Pat Loud

ASK YOUR CHILD WHAT HE WANTS FOR DINNER ONLY IF HE'S BUYING.

—FRAN LEBOWITZ

Truth, which is important to a scholar, has got to be concrete. And there is nothing more concrete than dealing with babies, burps and bottles, frogs and mud.

—Jeane J. Kirkpatrick

THERE NEVER WAS A CHILD SO LOVELY BUT HIS MOTHER WAS GLAD TO GET HIM ASLEEP.

—RALPH WALDO EMERSON

God knows that a mother needs fortitude and courage and tolerance and flexibility and patience and firmness and nearly every other brave aspect of the human soul. But because I happen to be a parent of almost fiercely maternal nature, I praise *casualness*. It seems to me the rarest of virtues. It is useful enough when children are small. It is important to the point of necessity when they are adolescents.

—Phyllis McGinley

Trying to be Supermom is as futile as trying to be Perfect Mum. Not going to happen.

—Arianna Huffington

[A successful parent is someone] who raises a child who grows up and is able to pay for his or her own psychoanalysis.

——Nora Ephron

The moment I learned I was pregnant in early 1993, life became all about the kid for me. I took the oath of our generation that I would not, would never, give my child any reason to mention my name in therapy.

—Terri Minsky

If you bungle raising your children,
**I don't think whatever else you do
well matters very much.**

—JACQUELINE KENNEDY ONASSIS

My mother used to say that her
proudest accomplishment was her four
children. For years, but especially as a
teenager, I would cringe every time I
heard this remark. "The poor woman
needs to get a life," I'd think.

—Beth Brophy

A suburban mother's role is to deliver children obstetrically once, and by car forever after.

—Peter De Vries

In the eyes of its mother every beetle is a gazelle.

—Moroccan proverb

But she named the infant 'Pearl,' as being of great price— purchased with all she had—her mother's only treasure!

—Nathaniel Hawthorne

Still, even though Donna Reed was my fantasy girl, I knew going in that I'd be cheating on her regularly. For all my nostalgia and revisionist stirrings, I was under no illusion about the stuff that happened off-camera: that there were times even a wonderful mother wanted to smack her kids and tell her husband to shut up.

—Lonnae O'Neal Parker

I WOULD HAVE MADE A TERRIBLE MOTHER. FOR ONE THING, I HATE TO REPEAT MYSELF.

—JOAN MANLEY

Every mother has a certain amount of "worry energy" to disperse into the world, and a child is an excellent, almost unavoidable, lightning rod for it.

—Harriet Lerner, PhD

A sweater is a garment worn by a child whose mother feels chilly.

—Barbara Johnson

My girlfriends got me … an in-car refrigerator so I can eat lunch in my car in the carpool lane. Because I'm obsessive. I'm the first person in the school line every day. **I'm compulsively early.**

—Jamie Lee Curtis

[T]here's no such thing as calling in sick
on mommyhood.

—COKIE ROBERTS

Then there are those [moms] who could do with
some distance, those "helicopter moms" who hover
over their children twenty-four hours a day, micro-
managing their worlds, turning the elementary
school play into auditions for Juilliard or Saturday
soccer into the pre-Olympics.

—Beth Brophy

*It's clear that most American children suffer
too much mother and too little father.*

—Gloria Steinem

Society is now influenced, shaped, and even to a large extent controlled by women. This is a far cry from the world of our childhood, when society was controlled by . . . Well, as the author recalls, society was controlled by Mum. Christmas dinner for all the relatives, square dancing, the PTA, split-level ranch houses with two and a half baths—surely no man thought these up.

—P. J. O'ROURKE

You never realize how much your mother loves you till you explore the attic—and find every letter you ever sent her, every finger painting, clay pot, bead necklace, Easter chicken, cardboard Santa Claus, paperlace Mother's Day card, and school report since day one.

—Pam Brown

Motherly love is not much use if it expresses itself only as a warm gush of emotion, delicately tinged with pink. It must also be strong, guiding, and unselfish. The sweetly sung lullaby, the cool hand on the fevered brow, the Mother's Day smiles and flowers are only a small part of the picture. True mothers have to be made of steel to withstand the difficulties that are sure to beset their children.

—Rachel Billington

118

My mother's influence in molding my character was conspicuous. She forced me to learn daily of chapters of the bible by heart. To that discipline and patient, accurate resolve I owe not only much of my general power of taking pains, but the best part of my taste for literature.

—John Ruskin

I make it a point with all of my kids
not to compliment them on their looks,
but on their achievements.
—CHRISTIE BRINKLEY

The biggest lesson we have to give
our children is truth.
—Goldie Hawn

Love and respect are the most important
aspects of parenting, and of all relationships.
—Jodie Foster

People always talked about a mother's uncanny ability to read her children, but that was nothing compared to how children could read their mothers.

—Anne Tyler

The thing that impresses me most about America is the way parents obey their children.

—Edward, Duke of Windsor

Parents were invented to make children happy by giving them **something to ignore.**

—Ogden Nash

Because I Said So: Mumisms

Sooner or later we all quote our mothers.
—Bern Williams

- If all your friends jumped off the roof, would you want to jump off the roof too?

- Yes, I am the boss of you.

- Eat your dinner—children are starving in the Third World.

- No dessert until you clean your plate.

- Don't give me that look. Do you want your face to freeze like that?

- You're not going out of the house dressed like that.

- Put on clean underwear. You never know when you might get hit by a bus.

- Look at me when I'm talking to you.

- Shut off that TV. It's too nice a day to sit inside.

- Clean up your room. You weren't raised in a barn.

- Don't make me tell you again.

- Take that out of your mouth. You don't know where it's been.

- Shut the door. We're not heating the whole outdoors.

- Money doesn't grow on trees.

- Just wait until you're the mother.

- Don't make me call your father.

- You'll thank me for this someday.

- Because I'm the mother.

- You'll be sorry when I'm gone.

It is not a bad thing that children should occasionally, and politely, put parents in their place.
— Colette

Parents of young children should realize that few people, and maybe no one, will find their children as enchanting as they do.

—Barbara Walters

There are only two things a child will share willingly—
communicable diseases and his mother's age.
—Dr. Benjamin Spock (attr.)

[P]arenthood is the most excruciatingly embarrassing job in the world. . . . Whatever subject embarrasses you most—your weight, the amount of money you make, the loudness of your snoring, the fact that you put ketchup on peanut butter sandwiches—consider it public knowledge.

—Sandi Kahn Shelton

Women know
The way to rear up children (to be just)
They know a simple, merry, tender knack
Of tying sashes, fitting baby-shoes
And stringing pretty words that make no sense.

—Elizabeth Barrett Browning

125

The best way to keep children home is
to make the home atmosphere pleasant—
and let the air out of the tires.

—DOROTHY PARKER

*A wise parent humors the desire
for independent action, so as to become the friend
and advisor when his absolute rule shall cease.*

—*Elizabeth Gaskell*

As a parent you try to maintain a certain
amount of control and so you have this tug-of-war....
You have to learn when to let go. And that's not easy.

—Aretha Franklin

It will be gone before you know it.
The fingerprints on the wall appear higher and higher.
Then suddenly they disappear.
                                    —Dorothy Evslin

THE SUCCESSFUL MOTHER
SETS HER CHILDREN FREE AND
BECOMES MORE FREE HERSELF
IN THE PROCESS.

                        —ROBERT J. HAVIGHURST

127

YOU SEE MUCH MORE
OF YOUR CHILDREN
ONCE THEY LEAVE HOME.

—LUCILLE BALL

No matter how old a mother is,
she watches her middle-aged children for signs
of improvement.

—Florida Scott-Maxwell

GROWN DON'T MEAN NOTHING TO A MOTHER. A CHILD IS A CHILD. THEY GET BIGGER, OLDER, BUT GROWN? WHAT'S THAT SUPPOSE TO MEAN? **IN MY HEART IT DON'T MEAN A THING.**

—TONI MORRISON, FROM *Beloved*

[M]y opinion is that the future good or bad conduct of a child depends on its mother.

—Letizia Ramolino Bonaparte, mother of Napoleon

For many, being the mother of an adult child was like having the final score recorded. Those who had "winning" results could finally stand back and take pride in how their children, to whom they had devoted themselves all these years, had turned out. They could look back and feel good about a job well done.

—Louis Genevie, PhD,
and Eva Margolies

A Complex Dynamic:

Mothers
and Daughters

A MOTHER'S TREASURE IS HER DAUGHTER.

—Catherine Pulsifer

Is my mother my friend? I would have to say, first of all she is my Mother, with a capital "M." She's something sacred to me. I love her dearly.... Yes, she is also a good friend, someone I can talk openly with if I want to.

—Sophia Loren

SOMETIMES YOU JUST NEED TO SPEAK TO YOUR MOTHER.

—Catherine Zeta-Jones

132

I never had a mother. I suppose a mother is one to whom you hurry when you are troubled.
—Emily Dickinson

MY MOM WOULD CRAWL OVER HOT COALS TO HAVE LUNCH WITH ME.
—COURTNEY THORNE-SMITH

Mummy herself has told us that she looked upon us more as her friends than her daughters. Now that is all very fine, but still, a friend can't take a mother's place. I need my mother as an example which I can follow, I want to be able to respect her.
—Anne Frank

Mama exhorted her children at every opportunity to "jump at de sun." We might not land on the sun, but at least we would get off the ground.

—Zora Neale Hurston

Mother, in a feminine way,

was ruthless. She was, in her own words, a jungle mother, and she knew too well that in a jungle it doesn't pay to be nice. "God will protect us," she often said to June and me. "But to make sure," she would add, "carry a heavy club."

—Gypsy Rose Lee

THE DOCTORS TOLD ME THAT
I WOULD NEVER WALK, BUT MY
MOTHER TOLD ME I WOULD,
SO I BELIEVED MY MOTHER.

—Wilma Rudolph,
Olympic gold medalist in track and field

It was my mother who gave me my voice. She did this, I know now, by clearing a space where my words could fall, grow, then find their way to others.

—Paula Giddings

135

What do girls do who haven't any mothers
to help them through their troubles?

—LOUISA MAY ALCOTT

Passing the Torch

Mum & Daughter, Inc. is on the rise.
According to the Center for Women's
Business Research, women own almost half of privately held companies
in the United States, and 37 percent
of female entrepreneurs intend to
pass their business on to a daughter.

SHE UNDERSTOOD
WHAT I WANTED
AND NEVER STOOD IN MY WAY.
—JADA PINKETT SMITH

[My mother] tried in every way to understand me, and she succeeded. It was this deep, loving understanding as long as she lived that more than anything else helped and sustained me on my way to success.

—Mae West

My mother drew a distinction
between achievement and success. She said that
"achievement is the knowledge that you have studied and worked hard and done the best that is in
you. Success is being praised by others, and that's
nice, too, but not as important or satisfying. Always
aim for achievement and forget about success."

—Helen Hayes

*My mother's best advice to me was:
"Whatever you decide to do in life, be sure that the
joy of doing it does not depend on the applause
of others, because in the long run we are, all of
us, alone."*

—Ali McGraw

138

I was also close to my mother and my grand-mother, my dad's mother. They gave me great values, and they had great confidence in me.

—Christie Hefner

My mom raised two champions, and there was a tremendous cost to that. Half-assed was never an option. And of course there's no such thing as perfection.

—WYNONNA JUDD

To describe my mother would be to write about a hurricane in its perfect power.

—Maya Angelou

My mother was a dominant force in my life.
She had a very specific idea about education, which was: You should know everything about everything. . . . I think that I
had a very eclectic and, in a way, a very democratic education. I'm grateful for that.

—TWYLA THARP

[M]y mother always told me that I was
going to go to college, even if she didn't have but one
dress to put on. So I grew up knowing that I was
going to somehow find a way out of the situation I
grew up in.

—Coretta Scott King

140

I was never allowed to read the popular American children's books of my day because, as my mother said, the children spoke bad English *without the author's knowing it.*

—Edith Wharton

I was a strict disciplinarian, perhaps too strict at times, but my God, without discipline what is life? I mean, how do you cope with life if you haven't enough self-discipline to cope with the problems and the games we have to face?

—JOAN CRAWFORD

Mother valued a sense of humor

and insisted that we develop one. More often than not, it was at our own expense. At first she'd point out some foolishness in our behavior and we'd be required to laugh, although I usually felt more like crying from embarrassment. By the time I was just eight or nine, I learned to laugh whether I felt like it or not because our mother could get quite provoked if you didn't see the humor as she saw it.

—Christina Crawford,
on her mother, Joan Crawford

Women who felt *less* accepted by their own mothers were *more* able to provide love for their children than women who felt their mothers loved and accepted them fully!

—Louis Genevie, PhD,
and Eva Margolies

I was lost without my mother. She had been my sounding board, my conscience. She was not the most affectionate person—in fact there were times when I thought she was cold—but she loved me in her heart, and I knew that all along.

—AUDREY HEPBURN

We in our forties have mostly learned to forgive our mothers for the crimes they committed in raising us. We have paid therapists thousands of dollars and spent endless hours talking with friends, going over and over the mistakes that were our legacy, and we have figured out how not to make the same errors with our daughters.

—Sandi Kahn Shelton

And it came to me, and I knew what I had to have before my soul would rest. I wanted to belong—to belong to my mother. And in return—I wanted my mother to belong to me.

—Gloria Vanderbilt

When I go home my mother and I play a cannibal game; we eat each other over the years, tender morsel by morsel, until there is nothing left but dry bone and wig.

—MAUREEN HOWARD

144

My mother was dead for five years before I knew that I had loved her very much.

—Lillian Hellman

The woman who bore me is no longer alive, but I seem to be her daughter in increasingly profound ways.

—Johnnetta Betsch Cole

[My grandmother] died when my mother was three months married, but her story is my mother's story. Together they chose my name when my mother was twelve, and referred to me as someone who would exist. Their story is so complex and layered and shot through with luminous sorrow that I will exist, and become a writer to make sure the stories don't vanish.

—Jayne Anne Phillips

When I stopped seeing my mother with the eyes of a child, I saw the woman who helped me give birth to myself.

—Nancy Friday

In my generation, many of us knew that we did not want to be like our mothers, even when we loved them. We could not help but see their disappointment. . . . Strangely, many mothers who loved their daughters—and mine was one—did not want their daughters to grow up like them either. They knew we needed something more.

—BETTY FRIEDAN

Mum Is *Always* Right

I was one of these kids who grew up not wanting to be my mom. Like, she was the stay-at-home mom and I was going to make something of my life. And the older I become, the more all I want is to be my mother. In the sense that she instilled in her children such strength of character and dignity and "do the right thing."

—Meredith Vieira

My mother wanted me to be her
wings, to fly as she never quite had the courage to do. I love her for that. I love the fact that she wanted to give birth to her own wings.

—Erica Jong

In many ways my mom, feminist author Erica Jong, anticipated the Generation X ideal of motherhood. She was successful, in her late thirties, and had both a book on the *Times* bestseller list and a nanny all lined up.

—Molly Jong-Fast

My mother says I have a lot of chutzpah. I did. You know, I was really naive about my career. I just figured if I kept working hard, and if I just seized moments, that things would happen, and that is really the way it worked.

—Sheryl Crow

The only thing that my mother and my sister and I wanted to do . . . was to come to New York and further our training. We got here, and we were, of course, typical tourists. Saw everything, did everything. . . . [M]y mother had realized that if we wanted to further our training and become professionals, we had to come to New York. **Fortunately, she was willing to come. She was more than happy to come.**

—Suzanne Farrell

We wore uniforms to school, but [my mother] made many of the rest of my sister's and my clothes, including our evening dresses when we were in high school. Sometimes she'd still be stitching us into our dresses, not having time to install a zipper, while our dates were downstairs getting grilled by Daddy. Years later, when we were no longer embarrassed, we teased her that she had devised **a wicked way to ensure our purity.**

—Cokie Roberts

I remember once one of my playmates from around the corner died, probably of leukemia. My mother took me to this funeral and took me up to see Rachel. And I saw Rachel's hands clasped over her chest, and her face was bloodless, and her hands were flat, and I was scared, because this was the little girl I used to play with. My mother leaned over to me and she said, "This is what happens when you don't listen to your mother."

—AMY TAN

My mother could make anybody feel guilty—she used to get letters of apology from people she didn't even know.

—Joan Rivers

My mother should have been Jewish. She could have taught a class on how to induce guilt.

—LORNA LUFT, DAUGHTER OF JUDY GARLAND

My mother gave me my drive but my father gave me my dreams.

—Liza Minnelli

Be a first-rate version of yourself, not a second-rate version of someone else.

—JUDY GARLAND, TO DAUGHTER LIZA MINNELLI

My mother's great. She has the major looks. She could stop you from doing anything, through a closed door even, with a single look. Without saying a word, she has that power to rip out your tonsils.

—Whoopi Goldberg

It's all right. That's my life. I really don't know what it's like not to have a famous mother.

—Mamie Gummer, on what it's like
to be Meryl Streep's daughter

THERE IS A POINT AT WHICH YOU AREN'T AS MUCH MOM AND DAUGHTER AS YOU ARE ADULTS AND FRIENDS.

—JAMIE LEE CURTIS

155

Raising daughters is different from raising sons.... If you have a daughter, trust me, from the time she is three weeks old, she is thinking, "Hmmm, this is the same sweater I spit up on last time. Doesn't this woman have any *variety* to her wardrobe?"

—Sandi Kahn Shelton

The mother–daughter dynamic that occurs between the generations is very complex and not very well understood.

—Louis Genevie, PhD, and Eva Margolies

156

As is the mother, so is her daughter.

—JOHN RUSKIN

Never say anything on the phone
that you wouldn't want your mother to hear at your trial.

—"*Mayflower Madam*"
Sydney Biddle Barrows

There is only one person an English girl hates more than she hates her elder sister; and that is her mother.

—George Bernard Shaw

Anyone who remembers their teen years will understand that at the age of fifteen, your mother's prominence is not nearly as important as your friends, your clothes, your hair! In the world of my peers, my mother's position as the advice queen was somewhere between cool and "who cares?" **Luckily for me, my mother never confused her work with her life.**

—Margo Howard on her mother, Ann Landers

158

To Emerson and all her friends, I'm just Mummy. I mean, believe me, as much as it seems like I'm a celebrity to you, the thing I'm known for is throwing kick-ass children's birthday parties.

—Teri Hatcher

My mom feels really famous to me. She's the most famous person I know. I think all moms feel famous.

—CLAIRE DANES

IN MY MOTHER'S HOUSE
THERE IS STILL GOD.

—LORRAINE HANSBERRY

159

Daughter I am in my mother's house;
But mistress in my own.

—Rudyard Kipling

Guided by my heritage of a love of

beauty and a respect for strength—in search of my
mother's garden, I found my own.

—Alice Walker

Thou art thy mother's glass, and she in thee
Calls back the lovely April of her prime.

—William Shakespeare

It's tough being compared to a great actress and a great beauty.

—NATASHA RICHARDSON,
SPEAKING OF HER MOTHER, VANESSA REDGRAVE

My mother is my mirror and I am hers. What do we see? Our face grown young again.
—*Marge Piercy*

O fairer daughter of a fair mother!

—Horace

A fluent tongue is the only thing a mother don't like her daughter to resemble her in.

—Richard Brinsley Sheridan

You Are What She Eats

A multitude of studies conclude that mothers are the single greatest influence on their daughters' eating habits and overall health. "Like mother, like daughter" holds true for eating fruits and vegetables, valuing exercise, and drinking milk. Similarly, mothers who pressure or coerce their daughters about food are more likely to have obese daughters, and mothers who diet repeatedly for rapid weight loss are likely to raise daughters who do the same.

[T]hese remarkable women of olden times are like the ancient painted glass—the art of making them is lost; my mother was less than her mother, and I am less than my mother.

—Harriet Beecher Stowe

My daughter is about to become a mother. Just to write that sentence down still seems to me joyful and incredible, though we have had eight months to get used to it.

—Ellen Goodman

I am an onlooker on my daughter's
dance, which I made possible because she
came through me. . . . I'm not a part of
her dance. Yet whenever she takes a pause
and needs someone to talk to, I am there.
But that special dance with the child and
the future is hers.

—LIV ULLMANN

*There came a moment quite suddenly
when a mother realized that a child was no longer
hers. . . . [W]ithout bothering to ask or even give
notice,* **her daughter had just grown up.**

—Alice Hoffman

NO WOMAN CAN SHAKE OFF HER
MOTHER. THERE SHOULD BE NO
MOTHERS, ONLY WOMEN.

—GEORGE BERNARD SHAW

My mother was very sick from the time I was born,
and died when I was fourteen. So I think my love of
books in some ways came from knowing that she
was pretty much bound to the home, and read all
the time as a way of learning about other worlds
that she would never be able to experience. . . . So
books took on a certain kind of magic for me.

—Doris Kearns Goodwin

Now that I'm a mother, I know more
what it was like to be her. I can't imagine what it
must have been like for her to be dying and have six
children. I can't imagine that feeling of leaving your
children and not knowing what's going to happen to
them. . . . I understand who my mother was by being
a mother. I guess I'm really only getting to know my
mother now.

—Madonna, on her mother's
dying when Madonna was six

But most of all, a mother teaches her daughter,
whether she plans to or not, about being a female person,
and whether that is a possible thing to be or whether it is
simply a contradiction in terms.

—Betty Carter

Born in Bed with a Lady:

Mothers and Sons

If a man has been his mother's undisputed darling, he retains throughout life the triumphant feeling, the confidence in success, which not seldom brings actual success with it.

—Sigmund Freud

We bear the world and we make it. . . . There was never a great man who had not a great mother— it is hardly an exaggeration.

—Olive Schreiner

When I was a child, my mother said to me, "If you become a soldier, you'll be a general. If you become a monk, you'll end up as the pope." Instead I became a painter and wound up as Picasso.

—Pablo Picasso

My father was poor.... He thought that with the music there was very little to do, and he thought better to be a carpenter. He was thinking seriously of that for me, but my mother said to him, "This boy has a gift, and it is our duty to follow it." **She was a wonderful woman.**

—Pablo Casals

For my confirmation, I didn't get a
watch and my first pair of long pants,
like most Lutheran boys. I got a telescope.
My mother thought it would make the
best gift.

—WERNHER VON BRAUN

[My mother] played a little guitar and piano, and
loved to sing. From the time I started trying to sing
when I was a kid, she always encouraged me to do
it. I told her when I was about twelve that I was
going to sing on the radio. **She encouraged
that dream.**

—Johnny Cash

Steven was not what you would call a good student. We had tutors schlep him through courses. Of course, there was a lot of absenteeism. If the kids didn't want to go to school, it was okay by me. Steven would do the thermometer on the lightbulb trick [like in *E.T.*] . . . I played along. Then, an hour later, Steven would perk up and say, "Let's go out in the desert and make films."

— Leah Adler, on her son Steven Spielberg

My MOTHER HAD A GREAT
DEAL OF TROUBLE WITH ME,
BUT I THINK SHE ENJOYED IT.

— MARK TWAIN

NOBODY CAN MISUNDERSTAND
A BOY LIKE HIS OWN MOTHER.
—NORMAN DOUGLAS (ATTR.)

[My mother] ... would watch me do my
stand-up comedy and make little notes. I'd
ask her how she liked the show. And she
would consult her notes, then actually say,
"You know, no one wants to see someone be
funny *all the time*." She'd say, "Why don't you
tell some jokes, then maybe sing a little song
... or do a little dance! Make it entertaining.
Nobody wants to hear jokes *all the time*."

—Jay Leno

I shall never forget my mother, for it was she who planted and nurtured the first seeds of good within me. She opened my heart to the lasting impressions of nature; she awakened my understanding and extended my horizon and her percepts exerted an everlasting influence upon the course of my life.

—IMMANUEL KANT

I recall having the ambition to study law, to be elected to Congress, and to try to make just laws, but I didn't pursue the study of law, for a curious reason. My mother didn't think I would make a very good lawyer. And I believe that her reasons were that I couldn't really win an argument with her.

—Jonas Salk, MD

At the time I was about to break a world record and become well known, my mother used to say, "Well, it is all right, this running business, but I hope it doesn't distract you from your work as a medical student."

—Sir Roger Bannister

My mother was my first and toughest audience. You know with mothers you have to "work the womb." Our connection was comedy. We're closest when we laugh. It's like Lenny Bruce once said, "Most comedians are driven by 'Love me!'" and mothers are the source.

—Robin Williams

She is my first, great love. She was a wonderful, rare woman—you do not know; as strong, and steadfast, and generous as the sun. She could be as swift as a white whiplash, and as kind and gentle as warm rain, and as steadfast as the irreducible earth beneath us.

—D. H. Lawrence

Who is it that loves me and will love me for ever with an affection which no chance, no misery, no crime of mine can do away? It is you, **my mother.**

—Thomas Carlyle

Few misfortunes can befall a boy which bring worse consequences than to have a really affectionate mother.

—W. Somerset Maugham

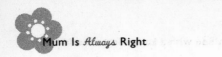

Mothers are warned that boys may become "effeminate" if we don't bow out of their lives, especially at adolescence. We're told that they need to be "separate" and tough and independent to find their way in the world of men. We're told boys shouldn't be like girls, or sons shouldn't be like their mothers. Later we turn around and say, "Hey! What's wrong with these guys? They can't relate."

—HARRIET LERNER, PhD

All women become like their mothers.
That is their tragedy. No man does. That's his.

—Oscar Wilde

My mother had dreams of being a writer, and I used to see her type in the front room. . . . Clearly she was making a heroic effort, and the things would go off in brown envelopes to New York or Philadelphia even, which had the [*Saturday Evening*] *Post* in those years, and they would come back. And so the notion of it being something that was worth trying and could, indeed, be done with a little postage and effort stuck in my head.

—John Updike

The writer's only responsibility is to his art. He will be completely ruthless if he is a good one. . . . If a writer has to rob his mother, he will not hesitate; the "Ode on a Grecian Urn" is worth any number of old ladies.

—William Faulkner

[M]y mother did not believe in television. We just didn't watch much of it. She just thought it was bad, and that was thirty years ago. She believed in books, and we were taught to read early. We were encouraged to read, throughout childhood and adolescence, by my mother.

—John Grisham

I knew that I wanted to be a writer from a very early age, because my mother was a writer, and encouraged me to write. I accepted that. I got it in my head. "Yeah, that's what I'm going to do. I'm going to be a writer."

—Scott Momaday

178

My mother, without doubt, was the source of my literary aspirations. When I was a child, she wanted to write. I felt her longing powerfully, the way children do, and it took root in me, well before I had any other reason to lay claim to literary ambitions—a kind of psychological version of those alien visit movies, where spores are planted in unsuspecting earthlings.

—Scott Turow

TO MY EMBARRASSMENT, I WAS BORN IN BED WITH A LADY.

—WILSON MIZNER

I saw pure love when my son looked at me, and I knew that I had to make a good life for the two of us.

—Suzanne Somers

I gave birth to [a son] more than twenty years ago, when I was only twenty myself, and didn't like men very much and hoped desperately I was giving birth to a girl. . . . It was an immense discovery for me, to find I didn't care that he was also a Boy. Later I discovered that Boy was something wonderful, too.

—SALLIE TISDALE

Because I feel that in the heavens above,

The angels, whispering one to another,

Can find among their burning tears of love,

None so devotional as that of "Mother,"

Therefore, by that dear name I have long called you,

You who are more than mother unto me.

—Edgar Allan Poe

[Y]ou just wanted to pull your hair out because you'd wish they would just be quiet for a minute, or sit, or even bake cookies or pick up their dishes or any of that, which never happened spontaneously. But then there were the fun times when honestly, they were so silly, the five all together, that you just laughed a lot because there was just so much exuberance and happiness. I learned a lot from having boys.

—Ann Romney, on having five sons

[My son] was an unusually charming baby. . . . There was one problem. He didn't look like me or my husband. After one too many mailman jokes, I took a curl from his first haircut to a salon and said, "I want this." The hairdresser looked dubious. I insisted. After that, people would say, "I see where he gets that beautiful red hair."

—Dawn Drzal

Nobody can have the soul of me.
My mother has had it, and nobody can have it again.
Nobody can come into my very self again, and breathe
me like an atmosphere.

—D. H. Lawrence

Button Up

Many of the sweaters worn by Mister Rogers on the popular television show *Mister Rogers' Neighborhood* were knitted by his mother.

183

[S]hortly after Zachary was born . . .
Zelig-like, he appeared throughout my
past. . . . I seemed to remember carrying
him to the podium as I collected my high
school diploma. I could almost remember holding him by one hand while holding a plastic cup of beer in the other at a
college fraternity party. And wasn't that
Zachary in his stroller on the family vacation to Florida when I was twelve?

—KATE MOSES

I was standing in the bathroom looking like a mean raccoon. My hair was piled loosely on my head, mascara ringed my eyes from the night before. "You look like hell," I said to the mirror. Suddenly, there was this little voice.... My son was staring up at me, his huge sea-blue eyes full of longing.... "You're the most beautiful woman in the world." The scary thing was that he meant it.

—Mona Gable

MY MOTHER WAS THE MOST BEAUTIFUL WOMAN I EVER SAW.

—GEORGE WASHINGTON

A BOY'S BEST FRIEND IS HIS MOTHER.

—ANTHONY PERKINS, AS NORMAN BATES IN *Psycho*

Looking back on my childhood . . .
I do not believe that I ever felt love for any mature
person, except my mother, and even her I did not
trust, in the sense that shyness made me conceal
most of my real feelings from her.

—George Orwell

I don't think we realized when we were growing
up what fine mysteries were plotted and written at our
kitchen table, but we all knew Mother was a good writer.
After all, who else could proofread a homework paper,
spruce up a college application essay, and help write an
entertaining "What I Did on My Summer Vacation" report
all in one evening?

—David Clark, on his mother, Mary Higgins Clark

A man loves his sweetheart the most, his wife the best, but his mother the longest.

—*Irish Proverb*

One of the very few reasons I had any respect for my mother when I was thirteen was because she would reach into the sink with her bare hands—*bare hands*—and pick up that lethal gunk and drop it into the garbage. To top that, I saw her reach into the wet garbage bag and fish around in there looking for a lost teaspoon. *Bare hands*—a kind of mad courage.

—Robert Fulghum

I tell him it's my job to embarrass him. He's always embarrassed. I guess, you know, your kids just want you to be like everybody else, don't they?

—SUSAN SARANDON, ON HER SON MILES

I have a sixteen-year-old son, so I'm a soccer mom. I stand on the sidelines and I hear the things parents are saying, so I want them to understand what it is their kids are feeling in any sports environment.

—BRANDI CHASTAIN, MEMBER OF OLYMPIC GOLD MEDAL U.S. SOCCER TEAM

If the phrase "soccer moms" has rapidly become part of the political lexicon, it may be because it is cleverly positioned at the intersection of several different trends—the rise of soccer as a middle-class pastime, the demanding lives of working women, the diversification of the suburbs, the popularity of the Dodge Caravan, and so on.

—Jacob Weisberg

[My mother] used to whip me when I was bad with switches, or a slipper called a mule. She'd give me a real good whipping sometimes, but I never resented it. She never did it out of cruelty....There was none of this: "This is going to hurt me more than it does you." There wasn't any of that foolishness. I knew that what she was doing, she thought was for my own good, and it was.

—Shelby Foote

My mother was a wit, but never a sentimental one. Once, when somebody in our house stepped on our cat's paw, she turned to the cat and said sternly, "I *told* you not to go around barefoot!"

—Zero Mostel

It takes a woman twenty years to make a man of her son, and another woman twenty minutes to make a fool of him.

—Helen Rowland

My mother wanted me to be a nice boy. I didn't let her down. I don't smoke, drink, or mess around with women.

—Julian Clary

MEN ARE WHAT THEIR
MOTHERS MADE THEM.

—RALPH WALDO EMERSON

God forgive us—but most of us grew up to be the sort of men our mothers warned us against.

—Brendan Behan

A wise son maketh a glad father; but a foolish son is the heaviness of his mother.

——Proverbs 10:1

The concept of "Momism" is male nonsense. It is the refuge of a man seeking excuses for his own lack of virility.

—Pearl Buck

Mothers all want their sons to grow up to become president, but they don't want them to become politicians in the process.

—JOHN F. KENNEDY

To me, **producing a great son** who is an inspiration to man is more exciting than writing a great book or producing a great painting.

—Rose Fitzgerald Kennedy

THE FUTURE DESTINY OF THE CHILD IS ALWAYS THE WORK OF THE MOTHER.

—NAPOLEON BONAPARTE

There seems to be a sort of presidential configuration—saintly mother, loutish father. You see the pattern in Ronald Reagan's parents back in Illinois, and, God knows, you see it in John Kennedy's—Mother Rose off to mass every morning (if not off to Paris to buy clothes), and Papa Joe off to Gloria Swanson's bed in Hollywood. Bill Clinton's mother, Virginia Kelley, though no saint in any sense that would impress Rome, had a saint's devotion to her boy.

—Lance Morrow

I think of her, two boys dying of tuberculosis,
nursing four others . . . **she was a saint.**
— Richard M. Nixon, *recalling his mother*

It was she who taught me to
get up every day and keep going; to look
for the best in people even when they saw
the worst in me; to be grateful for every
day and greet it with a smile; to believe I
could do or be anything I put my mind to
if I were willing to make the requisite
effort; to believe that, in the end, love
and kindness would prevail over cruelty
and selfishness.

—BILL CLINTON, ON HIS MOTHER

194

No one in the world can take the place of your mother. Right or wrong, from her viewpoint you are always right. She may scold you for little things, but never for the big ones.

—Harry Truman

ALL THAT I AM, OR HOPE TO BE,
I OWE TO MY ANGEL MOTHER.

—ABRAHAM LINCOLN

Mother always said that honesty was the best policy and money isn't everything. She was wrong about other things too.

—Gerald Barzan

Male Advantage

Statistically speaking, mothers are slightly more likely to have sons than daughters. The normal human birth ratio by gender is 1.05 males for 1.00 females. In other words, for every 100 girls born, there will be 105 boys.

It is odd how all men develop the notion, as they grow older, that their mothers were wonderful cooks. I have yet to meet a man who will admit that his mother was a kitchen assassin and nearly poisoned him.

—Robertson Davies

The most remarkable thing about my mother is that for thirty years she served the family nothing but leftovers. The original meal has never been found.

—Calvin Trillin

For years, since I was nine or ten, my mother had gone mad in the fall. I would start to see that look in her eyes, smell that odd aroma wafting off her skin. And I would know. I would always know before anyone else. I had been born with some kind of sonar that detected mental illness.

—Augusten Burroughs

I think God made a woman to be strong and not to be trampled under the feet of men. I've always felt this way because my mother was a very strong woman, without a husband.

—Little Richard

It seems to me that my mother was the most splendid woman I ever knew. . . . I have met a lot of people knocking around the world since, but I have never met a more thoroughly refined woman than my mother. If I have amounted to anything, it will be due to her.

—CHARLES CHAPLIN

I came from a broken home, so my mom was a major influence in my life. And I remember hearing her say hundreds, thousands of times, "You don't have to work that hard to try to be a good person, just do it." **Before "just do it" was fashionable.**

—Julius Erving

Fifty-four years of love and tenderness and crossness and devotion and unswerving loyalty. Without her I could have achieved a quarter of what I have achieved, not only in terms of success and career, but in terms of personal happiness. . . . She has never stood between me and my life, never tried to hold me too tightly, always let me go free.

—Noel Coward

In all my efforts to learn to read, my mother shared fully my ambition and sympathized with me and aided me in every way she could. If I have done anything in life worth attention, I feel sure that I inherited the disposition from my mother.

—Booker T. Washington

My mother really pushed for us, you know, to get a good education, and two things she always said was, you know, "You always have to be accountable for what you say and what you do." And the other thing she told me was that honesty and integrity had to define your character.

—Lenny Wilkens

I was a pretty good student. My mom wanted to emphasize that school was a very important part of my life. She wanted me to do well, and I took that message to heart.

—Kareem Abdul-Jabbar

My mother was the making of me. She was so true and so sure of me, I felt that I had someone to live for, someone I must not disappoint. The memory of my mother will always be a blessing to me.

—THOMAS A. EDISON

Is it so strange that boys who grow up with too much mother love become men who can never get enough?

—Betty Friedan

A man loves his sweetheart the most, his wife the best, **but his mother the longest.**

—Irish proverb

THE OLDER I BECOME, THE MORE I THINK ABOUT MY MOTHER.

—INGMAR BERGMAN

Sometimes I feel that my mother alone really knows who I am—the furtive boy, the trespasser, the secret wanker in his room.

—JAMES ATLAS

A man never sees all that his mother has been to him until it's too late to let her know that he sees it.

—William Dean Howells

In the man whose childhood has known caresses, there is always a fibre of memory that can be touched to gentle issues.

—George Eliot

SONS ARE THE ANCHORS
OF A MOTHER'S LIFE.
—Sophocles

It has taken me the time since you died
to discover you are as human as I am . . .
if I am.

—Robert Lowell

Guilt Is Her Middle Name:

Mothers and Work

NOW, AS ALWAYS, THE
MOST AUTOMATED APPLIANCE IN
A HOUSEHOLD IS THE MOTHER.

—BEVERLY JONES

You never know in retrospect whether
you did or didn't do exactly the right
thing, stay-at-home mothers, gone-
away mothers, all of us worry whether
we should have done something differ-
ently than we did.

—HILLARY RODHAM CLINTON

Women's rights in essence is really a movement for freedom, a movement for equality, for the dignity of all women, for those who work outside the home and those who dedicate themselves with more altruism than any profession I know to being wives and mothers, cooks and chauffeurs, and child psychologists and loving human beings.

—Jill Ruckelshaus

THE PHRASE
"WORKING MOTHER"
IS REDUNDANT.

—JANE SELLMAN

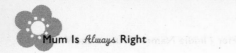

"Working mother" is a misnomer. . . . It implies that any mother without a definite career is lolling around eating bon-bons, reading novels, and watching soap operas. But the word "mother" is already a synonym for some of the hardest, most demanding work ever shouldered by any human. . . . It can be failure or triumph, but it can never be insignificant or unimportant since it is one "job" affecting the outcome of another's life.

—Liz Smith

I looked on child-rearing not only as a work of love and duty but as a profession that was fully as interesting and challenging as any honorable profession in the world and one that demanded the best that I could bring to it.

—Rose Fitzgerald Kennedy

I don't think that all good mothers have to bake and sew and make beds and wear percale bungalow aprons. Some of the finest never go into their kitchens at all.

—Kathleen Norris

Being a full-time mother is one of the highest-salaried jobs . . . since the payment is pure love.

—Mildred B. Vermont

All mothers are

WORKING MOTHERS.

—Unknown

209

God used to be a mother who worked outside the home. For thousands of years—from the Old Stone Age to the closing of the last goddess temples, about A.D. 500—She did it all. The Great Mother, as She came to be called, gave birth, underwent transformation, death, rebirth, and everything in between, and She caused mortals to do the same.

—Shari L. Thurer

I'm a mom and I've told my children
that being a mom is the most important job and I've shown them that by being home for six years. But I also want to be a mentor for them and a role model for them as a career person because that is a part of me and I hope that . . . they have a passion for something the way I have a passion for news.

—Kim Khazei, Boston local TV news anchor

I need to work for my spiritual and emotional well-being, and while that might not be admirable, it's true. In interim periods between jobs I've suffered genuine depression, and believe me, it's not good for the children. I was a better mother because I worked.

—Cokie Roberts

My mom, a Radcliffe graduate and one of the smartest women I know, sipped rum and Coke from a little glass starting at 5 p.m. every day, threw shoes at us from across the living room, and at times became unhinged by the frustrations of staying home raising four children.

—Leslie Morgan Steiner

Majority Mums

Mums on the job are more the norm than stay-at-home moms. According to the Center for Policy Alternatives, 63 percent of mothers of small children and 78 percent of mothers of school-age children work outside the home.

If someone wanted to paint a portrait of my mother, he would have been wise to paint her at her desk. Where she was happiest.

—Mary Gordon

At work, you think of the children you have left at home. At home, you think of the work you've left unfinished. Such a struggle is unleashed within yourself. Your heart is rent.

—Golda Meir

I think while all mothers deal with feelings of guilt, **working mothers are plagued by guilt on steroids.**

—Arianna Huffington

With all the efforts made by modern society to nurture and educate the young, how stupid it is to permit the mothers of young children to spend themselves in the coarser work of the world!

—Jane Addams

For every woman, guilt is her middle name. I don't think women who spend their time with children should be made to feel guilty for "not using their brains," and I don't think women who work full-time should be made to feel guilty about not spending enough time with their children.

—Madeleine Albright

It's an old trick now, God knows, but it works every time. At the very moment women start to expand their place in the world, scientific studies deliver compelling reasons for them to stay home.

—Mary Kay Blakely

The causes of youth violence are working parents who put their kids into daycare, the teaching of evolution in the schools, and working mothers who take birth control pills.

—Tom DeLay

I'm always on the lookout for research "proving" that women who work are a) in the majority (because misery loves company); b) raising more, not fewer Nobel Prize winners or Olympic medalists; and c) not handicapping children for life, because they need or want to work.

—MELINDA M. MARSHALL

All we know is that the school achievement, IQ test score, and emotional and social development of working mothers' children are every bit as good as that of children whose mothers do not work.

—Sandra Scarr

I'm real ambivalent about [working mothers]. Those of us who have been in the women's movement for a long time know that we've talked a good game of "go out and fulfill your dreams" and "be everything you were meant to be." But by the same token, we want daughters-in-law who are going to stay home and raise our grandchildren.

—Erma Bombeck

Both at-home and working mothers can overmeet their mothering responsibilities. In order to justify their jobs, working mothers can overnurture, overconnect with, and overschedule their children into activities and classes. Similarly, some at-home mothers . . . can make at-home mothering into a bigger deal than it is, overstimulating, overeducating, and overwhelming their children with purposeful attention.

—Jean Marzollo

There was no appreciable difference in guilt between parents that worked outside the home and those that called themselves full-time, stay-at-home moms. The "SAHMs" told us that they feel guilty about the amount of time they spend doing the household management parts of their jobs, like cleaning and bill-paying, and not playing with the children. All moms everywhere feel guilty about working too much.

—Julie Bort, co-author of *Mommy Guilt*

YOU HAVE A LIFETIME TO WORK, BUT CHILDREN ARE ONLY YOUNG ONCE.

—POLISH PROVERB

There is a war going on in the streets of New York City. Platoons of mothers in bicycle shoes and designer sweats wheel divisions of gleaming, clanking strollers down the sidewalks, chattering into their cell phones and blocking the passage of other pedestrians. Their adversaries, the Working Mothers and the Women Without Children, straighten their sleek success suits and try to stay out of the way.

—Susan Cheever

Why is there this catfight between working mothers and stay-at-home moms? Despite the snarling most of us witness at times (and engage in ourselves), aren't we moms ultimately united in our quest to stay sane, raise good kids, provide one another with succor and support, and protect humankind from the overly aggressive, overly logical male half of the species?

—Leslie Morgan Steiner

219

Working motherhood has on various occasions made me feel tense, elated, exhausted, thrilled, bored, and sometimes angry. What it hasn't made me feel is guilty. Or, let me put it this way: If being a working mother makes me feel guilty about anything, it's about not feeling guilty.

—SARA NELSON

To nourish children and raise them against odds is any time, any place, more valuable than to fix bolts in cars or design nuclear weapons.
—Marilyn French

It's really important to let every woman find her way. And it would be great to support their decisions, whether it's to take two years off or to take six weeks off. Working mothers have a hard enough time as it is, wearing a zillion hats and juggling all these balls, and meeting a lot of people's expectations. What we don't need to do is pile on more pressure, and insist that she do it the way we would do it. **Let her figure out the best way for her.**

—Elizabeth Vargas

Being a housewife and a mother is the biggest job in the world, but, if it doesn't interest you, don't do it—I would have made a terrible mother.

—Katharine Hepburn

To me, it is clear that the brightest people are spread over all sorts of other occupations. Motherhood is likely among them, and why not? I was a stay-at-home mom while my children were small, and I loved it.

—Marilyn vos Savant

Working mothers are just as likely to want to conform to a standard of perfection—and just as likely to suffer from their failure to meet it—as their stay-at-home counterparts.

—Melinda M. Marshall

Cleaning house while your kids are still growing
Is like shoveling the walk before it stops snowing.
—Phyllis Diller

No one ever died from sleeping in an unmade bed. I have known mothers who remake the bed after their children do it because there's a wrinkle in the spread or the blanket is on crooked. This is sick.
—Erma Bombeck

The role of mother is probably the most important career a woman can have.
—JANET MARY RILEY

It takes more time than I care to give to my career. I have enormous responsibilities at home—I have four kids, and that's a big job.

—MERYL STREEP

What is sad for women of my generation is that they weren't supposed to work if they had families. What were they going to do when the children are grown—watch the raindrops coming down the window pane?

—Jacqueline Kennedy Onassis

Aside from those politically correct people who correct people when they say they no longer work—you do work, it's just at home—most people don't give stay-at-home moms their due. In the working world you get reviews, bonuses, your boss telling you a job well done. At home you get none of this.... The only concrete feedback you're going to get ... is spit, throw-up, and poop.

—Amy Einhorn

So much of society is about measuring success—I closed that deal, won that case, got that contract. If we can't measure it, we can't value it. As a mother, you can't see the results of your work for years. So much of it is intangible, but that does not mean that it is any less important than any kind of job or title of any kind.

—Jane Clayson

I look back on *A Fish Called Wanda* . . . without question one of my biggest successes. . . . What I remember was that my daughter was a baby, six months old. There were often days I'd come home and she was asleep already. And I thought, "What the frick am I doing?"

—JAMIE LEE CURTIS

It's definitely a struggle. You're pulled in so many directions, and you want to do 100 percent everywhere.

—Jennifer Garner,
on balancing career and motherhood

226

The other day something happened that I had been dreading for a long time. I came home from work in the evening and Judy, my son's nanny, handed him to me, as she does every day. My little darling six-month-old Owen gave me a perfunctory smile, patted me on the shoulder with his chubby hand, and then reached back for Judy.

—Kristin van Ogtrop

[P]eople in positions of power have no idea how complex, subtle, and highly skilled the job of full-time parent is. People tend to think of it as babysitting, and that's only because they have never done it.

—Ann Crittenden

227

Though motherhood is the most important of all the professions—requiring more knowledge than any other department in human affairs—there was no attention given to preparation for this office.

—Elizabeth Cady Stanton

Foremost among the barriers to equality is the system which ignores the mother's service to Society in making a home and rearing children. The mother is still the unchartered servant of the future, who receives from her husband, at *his* discretion, a share in *his* wages.

—Katharine Anthony

228

Swift Return

According to the U.S. Department of Labor Statistics, one-third of mothers return to work within three months of giving birth.

Clearly society has a tremendous stake in insisting on a woman's natural fitness for the career of mother: the alternatives are all too expensive.

—Ann Oakley

Any mother could perform the jobs of several air-traffic controllers with ease.

—LISA ALTHER

The only difference between men and women is that women are able to create new little human beings in their bodies while simultaneously writing books, driving tractors, working in offices, planting crops—in general, doing everything men do.

—Erica Jong

230

I HAVE A BRAIN AND A UTERUS,
AND I USE BOTH.

—PATRICIA SCHROEDER,
RESPONDING TO A QUESTION ABOUT
HOW SHE COULD BE A MOTHER AND A LAWMAKER

Having five children in six years is the best training in the world for Speaker of the House.

—Nancy Pelosi

I myself have been thankful for the opportunity to experience a rich and fulfilling career as well as a close and supportive family life. I know the lessons I have learned in each have aided me in the other. As a result, I can revel both in the growth of my granddaughter and in the legal subtleties of the Free Exercise Clause.

—Sandra Day O'Connor

Getting people to play well together! Some things are similar to children arguing and feeling that they can't understand the other person's side. You really would stop kids and say, "Try to figure out why the other person cares so much about that toy."

—Madeleine Albright, on the aspects of child-raising
that prepared her to be Secretary of State

Mums are resourceful. We can make any school project rate an A-plus with gaffer's tape and five toothpicks. We can end a screaming match amongst siblings with microwave popcorn, juice boxes, and a remote control. We can buy a half hour of world peace using only sidewalk chalk and bubbles.

—Susan Konig

At my children's school, there are mothers who
hold meetings with administrators to discuss the
juice policy. I would put a fork in my eye if that
were my life. But I'm grateful ... and I would like
to think that somehow, I'm returning the favor.
No, not by writing a television show for their children to watch. But maybe by letting their children
know they can someday turn the trauma of their
teenage years into an interesting career.

—Terri Minsky

If you can manage a group of small children, you can manage
a group of bureaucrats. It's almost the same process.

—Corporate executive quoted in
the Wellesley College report
"Inside Women's Power"

We may be doing our mothering, these days, in between performing brain surgery or addressing the United Nations, but in the overall context of our several million years of evolution from nonhuman primates to humans—during which the brains we have today took shape—**there is no other time when we need to be so smart.**

—Katherine Ellison

If evolution really works,
how come mothers only have two hands?
—Milton Berle

Working mothers are guinea
pigs in a scientific experiment
to show that sleep is not
necessary to human life.

—Unknown

Most baby books also tend to romanticize
the mother who stays at home, as if she
really spends her entire day doing nothing
but beaming at the baby and whipping up
educational toys from pieces of string,
rather than balancing cooing time with
laundry, cleaning, shopping, and cooking.

—SUSAN CHIRA

I used to put [my daughter] into the pushchair and walk her around Edinburgh, wait until she nodded off, and then hurry to a cafe and write as fast as I could. It's amazing how much you can get done when you know you have very limited time. I've probably never been as productive since, if you judge by words per hour.

—J. K. Rowling, on writing the first Harry Potter book

A man's work is from sun to sun, but a mother's work is never done.
—Unknown

I think we're seeing in working mothers a change from "Thank God it's Friday" to "Thank God it's Monday." If any working mother has not experienced that feeling, her children are not adolescent.

—Ann Diehl

No one but doctors and mothers
know what it means to have interruptions.
—Karl A. Menninger

Perhaps the greatest social service that can
be rendered by anybody to the country
and to mankind is to bring up a family.
But here again, because there is nothing
to sell, there is a very general disposition
to regard a married woman's work as no
work at all; and to take it as a matter of
course that she should not be paid for it.

—George Bernard Shaw

*A vacation frequently means that the family goes away
for a rest, accompanied by a mother, who sees
that the others get it.*

—Marcelene Cox

A MOTHER WHO IS REALLY
A MOTHER IS NEVER FREE.

—HONORÉ DE BALZAC

By and large, mothers and housewives are the only workers who do not have regular time off. They are the great vacationless class.

—Anne Morrow Lindbergh

Take motherhood: Nobody ever thought of putting it on a moral pedestal until some brash feminists pointed out, about a century ago, that the pay is lousy and the career ladder nonexistent.

—BARBARA EHRENREICH

IF MOTHERHOOD IS AN OCCUPATION WHICH IS CRITICALLY IMPORTANT TO SOCIETY THE WAY WE SAY IT IS, THEN THERE SHOULD BE A MOTHER'S BILL OF RIGHTS.

—BARBARA ANN MIKULSKI

One Jungle Between:

Mothers-in-Law

If you have a mother-in-law with only one eye and she has it in the center of her forehead, don't keep her in the living room.

—Lyndon B. Johnson

Quite nice women suddenly have to wear this title with the stigma on it and a crown of thorns. We're so frightened of it that we change our nature to avoid it and in so doing we end up the classical mother-in-law we feared in the first place; so gravely have we twisted ourselves.

—Sylvia Ashton-Warner

Happy Holidays

According to a survey conducted in the United Kingdom by Travelodge, almost one Brit in five dreads a Christmas visit by a mother-in-law more than any other relative.

Conscience is a mother-in-law

whose visit never ends.
—H. L. Mencken

Just got back from a pleasure trip:
I took my mother-in-law to the airport.
—Henny Youngman

243

Be kind to your mother-in-law,
but pay for her board at some good hotel.
—Josh Billings

[Pakistan is] the sort of place
everyone should send his mother-in-law
for a month, all expenses paid.
—IAN BOTHAM, BRITISH CRICKETEER

What a marvelous place
to drop one's mother-in-law!
—Marshal Ferdinand Foch,
on the Grand Canyon

(His)
Mother Knows Best

When divorce rates in Korea rose to the third highest in the world (after the United States and United Kingdom), a representative of the nation's family courts explained that disagreements between the mother-in-law and the wife were now the main cause of divorce there.

First, there is the rocket-boosted mother-in-law ... queen of the melodrama when her acts of self-sacrifice and martyrdom go unnoticed and unrewarded. Her banner is the tear-stained hanky. She is as phony as a colic cure, transparent as a soap bubble. And as harmless as a barracuda. **But she is really more wretched than wicked and needs more help than she can give.**

—Abigail Van Buren

I haven't spoken to my mother-in-law for eighteen months—I don't like to interrupt her.

—Ken Dodd

Never rely on the glory of the morning
nor the smiles of your mother-in-law.
— *Japanese proverb*

Then, there's the modern mother-in-law.
In her mid-forties, she is the compact car
of her breed: efficient, trim, attractive, and
in harmony with her times. . . . She's pretty
stiff competition for the plain young ma-
tron who's overweight and underfinanced.
If there is going to be friction in this relationship, it could start from envy and resentment in the younger woman. But Father
Time is on her side, even if Mother Nature
played her a dirty trick.

—ABIGAIL VAN BUREN

247

MY MOTHER-IN-LAW BROKE UP MY
MARRIAGE. MY WIFE CAME HOME
FROM WORK ONE DAY AND FOUND US
IN BED TOGETHER.

—LENNY BRUCE

I was staying in Cokie's girlhood room ... and at some point
I heard a knock on the door. Since this was 1963, I pretty
much figured it wasn't Cokie. The door opened and there
stood my future mother-in-law dressed in this flowing peach
negligee.... And she whispered, "Now, darling, you sound
terrible, drink this." ...The family joke is that I fell in love
with my mother-in-law first, and then got around to Cokie!

—Steve Roberts, on his future
mother-in-law's homemade cold remedy

Go not empty unto thy mother-in-law.

—BOOK OF RUTH 3:17

Behind every successful man stands a surprised mother-in-law.

—*Hubert H. Humphrey*

The mother-in-law thinks I'm effeminate: not that I mind that because, **beside her, I am!**

—LES DAWSON

Of all the peoples whom I have studied, from city dwellers to cliff dwellers, I always find that at least 50 percent would prefer to have at least one jungle between themselves and their mothers-in-law.

—MARGARET MEAD

Queen of the Hive

In traditional Afghan culture, the mother-in-law is at the pinnacle of a household's hierarchy, ranking above all of her daughters-in-law and her own daughters.

A person often catches a cold when a mother-in-law comes to visit. Patients mentioned mothers-in-law so often that we came to consider them a common cause of disease in the United States.

—Thomas Holmes

I TOLD MY MOTHER-IN-LAW
THAT MY HOUSE WAS HER HOUSE,
AND SHE SAID, "GET THE
HELL OFF MY PROPERTY."

—JOAN RIVERS

251

I saw six men kicking and punching the mother-in-law. My neighbour said 'Are you going to help?' I said 'No, six should be enough.'

—Les Dawson

I should, many a good day, have blown my brains out, but for the recollection that it would have given pleasure to my mother-in-law; and even *then*, if I could have been certain to haunt her . . .

—Lord Byron

But there, everything has its drawbacks, as the man said when his mother-in-law died and they came down upon him for the funeral expenses.

—Jerome K. Jerome

They say the definition of ambivalence is watching your mother-in-law drive over a cliff in your new Cadillac.

—David Mamet

Two mothers-in-law.

—Lord John Russell,
on the appropriate punishment for bigamy

ADAM WAS
THE LUCKIEST MAN;
HE HAD NO MOTHER-IN-LAW.
—MARK TWAIN

Greatest Cook
in the World:

Grandmothers

If becoming a grandmother was only a
matter of choice, I should advise every
one of you straight away to become one.
There is no fun for old people like it!

—HANNAH WHITALL SMITH

BECOMING A GRANDMOTHER
IS WONDERFUL. ONE MOMENT
YOU'RE JUST A MOTHER. THE
NEXT YOU ARE ALL-WISE AND
PREHISTORIC.

—PAM BROWN

A grandmother is a babysitter who watches the kids instead of the television.

—Unknown

Though I was a mother at twenty-one, being a grandmother makes the whole thing absolutely normal and gorgeous. The relief, the joy of being a grandmother is wonderful.

—Joanna Lumley

Mum Is *Always* Right

I DON'T FEEL LIKE A GRANDMOTHER.
I DON'T.

—PRISCILLA PRESLEY

It is as grandmothers that our mothers
come into the fullness of their grace.
—Christopher Morley

My grandmother was a Jewish juggler;
she used to worry about six things at once.
—Richard Lewis

258

A grandmother is a little bit parent, a little bit teacher, and a little bit best friend.

—Unknown

You have to stay in shape.
My grandmother started walking five miles a day when she was sixty. She's ninety-seven now, and we don't know where the hell she is.

—ELLEN DEGENERES

What in heaven's name is strange about a grandmother dancing nude? **I'll bet lots of grandmothers do it.**

—Sally Rand

259

When grandparents enter the door, discipline flies out the window.

—Ogden Nash

Most grandmas have a touch of the scallywag.

—Helen Thomson

Now that my mother has retired, she spends a lot of time with my sister's young children. Last night she called to tell me that she was dancing with my ten-month-old niece, Daisy, in her arms, singing to a Rod Stewart album....When the song ended, the baby said "Nana" and rested her head on my mother's shoulder. "It was better than an orgasm," my mother told me.

—Leslie Lehr

Under One Roof

According to the U.S. Census Bureau, 3.7 million grandmothers live with their grandchildren in the United States.

My grandmother sang, too, and she was really loud. It was this wild kind of singing. I count her among my influences.

—CASSANDRA WILSON

I dig being a mother. And, of course, as a grandmother, **I just run amok.**

—Whoopi Goldberg

JUST ABOUT THE TIME A WOMAN
THINKS HER WORK IS DONE, SHE
BECOMES A GRANDMOTHER.

—EDWARD H. DRESCHNACK

Soon I will be an old, white-haired lady, into whose lap someone places a baby, saying, "Smile, Grandma!" —I, who myself so recently was photographed on my grandmother's lap.

—Liv Ullmann

262

If I had known how wonderful it would
be to have grandchildren, **I'd have
had them first.**

—LOIS WYSE

IT'S ONE OF NATURE'S WAYS
THAT WE OFTEN FEEL CLOSER
TO DISTANT GENERATIONS
THAN TO THE GENERATION
IMMEDIATELY PRECEDING US.

—IGOR STRAVINSKY

I USED TO LISTEN TO THE SOAP OPERAS WITH MY GRANDMOTHER.

—BOB EDWARDS

My clearest memory of my Italian grandparents is that I never knew what they were talking about. My grandmother spoke no English at all, just what sounded like gibberish. The only words I could ever make out were "Jamie!" and "Gooood-a boy!" and "Here's a dollar!"

—Jay Leno

Grandma Sally taught me how to listen to my inner voice, and I guarantee you that even today, I take time to do just that.

—ROBIN ROBERTS

A grandmother is a mother who has a second chance.

—Unknown

I wonder if there is a grandparent pheromone or instinct that goes unmentioned in the DNA research. There must be some chemistry that turns adults with opera subscriptions and espresso machines into people who put bumper stickers on their cars that say: ASK ME ABOUT MY GRANDCHILDREN.

—ELLEN GOODMAN

265

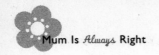

I'm not a picture-toting grandma—
but my grandsons, Tyler J. Phillips and
Dean Phillips, just happen to be the
best-looking, smartest, best-mannered
grandchildren in the continental United
States—and you can throw in Canada
and the Virgin Islands.

—ABIGAIL VAN BUREN

*I fear the seventh granddaughter
and the fourteenth grandchild becomes a very
uninteresting thing—for it seems to me to go on
like the rabbits in Windsor Park.*

—Queen Victoria

266

We have five sons, lovely sons, and ten grandchildren. I had to wait until my first granddaughter. **Finally I got to buy pink!**

—Ann Romney

My grandmother gave me the foundation for success that I was allowed to continue to build upon. My grandmother taught me to read, and that opened the door to all kinds of possibilities for me.

—OPRAH WINFREY

My grandmother played with me on the floor with blocks when I was eight years old in Canada, and she got cuttings for her wood stove from the shop. They were like bandsaw and jigsaw cuttings, and they were odd shapes, and we used to play, make fantasy cities.

—Frank Gehry,
on his early interest in architecture

Everyone needs access both to grand-parents and grandchildren in order to be a **full human being.**

—MARGARET MEAD

I was a mute from the time I was seven and a half until I was almost thirteen. . . . My grandmother, who was raising me in a little village in Arkansas, used to tell me, "Sister, mamma don't care about what these people say: 'You must be an idiot, you must be a moron.' . . . Mamma know, when you and the Good Lord get ready, you're gonna be a preacher."

—Maya Angelou

I had two grandmothers, and both were storytellers. . . . I think that I became a writer because I heard those stories—all the stories that I didn't know about Mexico, about my own land. They were the storehouse of these great tales of migrants, revolution, highway robberies, bandits, love affairs, ways of dressing, eating—they had the whole storehouse of the past in their heads and their hearts.

—Carlos Fuentes

You do not really understand something
unless you can explain it to your grandmother.
—Albert Einstein (attr.)

Uncles and aunts and cousins are all very well, and fathers and mothers are not to be despised; but a grand-mother, at holiday time, is worth them all.

—Fanny Fern

By December I'm in deep Xmas psychosis, and only then do I allow myself the luxury of daydreaming my favorite childhood memory: dashing through the snow, laughing all the way (ha-ha-ha) to Grandma's house to find that the fully decorated tree has fallen over and pinned her underneath.

—John Waters

A HOUSE NEEDS A
GRANDMA IN IT.
—LOUISA MAY ALCOTT

I bought a house in the Hollywood Hills and brought my grandmother from Harlem to live in it with me.

—Sammy Davis Jr.

As a child I knew almost nothing, nothing beyond what I had picked up in my grandmother's house. All children, I suppose, come into the world like that, not knowing who they are.

—V. S. Naipaul

Mum Is *Always* Right

We should all have one person who
knows how to bless us despite the evidence.
Grandmother was that person to me.

—PHYLLIS THEROUX

Perfect love sometimes does not come until
the first grandchild.

—Welsh proverb

Why do grandparents and grandchildren
get along so well? They have the same
enemy—the mother.

—CLAUDETTE COLBERT

272

A mother becomes a true grandmother the day she stops noticing the terrible things her children do because she is so enchanted with the wonderful things her grandchildren do.

—Lois Wyse

I guess I had it made. My mother gave me advice—she taught me that women like to be looked in the eye—and my grandmother gave me condoms.

—USHER

My grandmother used to say, "Make sure you look good. Make sure you speak well. Make sure you remain that Southern gentleman that I've taught you to be."

—Jamie Foxx

TO REFORM A MAN, YOU MUST
START WITH HIS GRANDMOTHER.

—VICTOR HUGO

If a grandmother wants to put her foot down,
the only safe place to do it these days is in a notebook.

—*Florida Scott-Maxwell*

A conservative is someone who makes
no changes and consults his grandmother
when in doubt.

—WOODROW WILSON

A Stitch in Time

Many women of all ages and family status (and a lot of men as well) make pieced quilts, but as a folk art, the quilt has long been associated with grandmothers. Even the names of many patterns reflect her role: Grandmother's Flower Garden (a hexagonal patchwork), Grandmother's Fan (clusters of five-sided "blades"), and the complex and lovely Grandmother's Engagement Ring (a variant of the Double Wedding Ring trousseau quilt).

*If nothing is going well,
call your grandmother.*
—*Italian proverb*

WHEN I WAS FOUR YEARS OLD,
MY GRANDMOTHER GOT ME ONE
OF THESE TOY PLASTIC GUITARS.
—KENNY WAYNE SHEPHERD

**A garden of love grows in a
Grandmother's heart.**
—Unknown

My grandmother was the greatest cook in the world. She could just go in there, the whole kitchen would look like a tornado hit it, and then she'd come out with the best food. Then she'd sit at the table and she wouldn't eat.

—EDIE BRICKELL

Being pretty on the inside means you don't hit your brother and you eat all your peas—that's what my grandma taught me.

—Lord Chesterfield

The best ally you can have in breaking up a street fight is a grandmother.

—JOE BOB BRIGGS

A grandma's name is little less in love than is the doting title of a mother.

—William Shakespeare

A GRANDMOTHER PRETENDS SHE DOESN'T KNOW WHO YOU ARE ON HALLOWEEN.

—ERMA BOMBECK

Changing a diaper is a lot like getting a present from your grandmother—you're not sure what you've got but you're pretty sure you're not going to like it.

—Jeff Foxworthy

Mothers and mothers-in-law can tell you some home truths about yourself and your spouse as you embark on bringing up those boisterous babies. Grandmothers can tell you some truths about your mother as well.

—COKIE ROBERTS

When a child is born, so are grandmothers.

—JUDITH LEVY

We have become a grandmother.
                              —*Margaret Thatcher*

Now that I've reached the age, or maybe the stage, where I need my children more than they need me, I really understand how grand it is to be a grandmother.

                              —Margaret Whitlam

Selected Biographical Notes

Jane Addams (1860–1935), social worker, feminist and first American woman to receive the Nobel Peace Prize.

Madeleine Albright (b. 1937), U.S. secretary of state under President Bill Clinton.

Louisa May Alcott (1832–1888), author of *Little Women*.

Maya Angelou (b. 1928), poet, historian, author, actress, playwright and civil rights activist.

Susan B. Anthony (1820–1906), reformer who fought for abolition of slavery and for women's right to vote.

Sarah Bird (b. 1949), novelist and journalist known for sharp wit and sense of the absurd.

Erma Bombeck (1927–1996), humor columnist who specialized in family observations.

Edie Brickell (b. 1966), singer and songwriter who rose to fame with the band the New Bohemians.

Heywood Broun (1888–1939), journalist, sportswriter, founder of the Newspaper Guild, and member of the Algonquin Round Table.

Pearl S. Buck (1892–1973), American novelist who won both the Pulitzer Prize for fiction and the Nobel Prize for literature.

Carol Burnett (b. 1936), television performer known for sketch comedy.

Lillian Carter (1898–1983), mother of former U.S. president Jimmy Carter.

Willa Cather (1873–1947), American fiction writer.

Susan Cheever (b. 1943), novelist, memoirist, and nonfiction author.

Agatha Christie (1890–1976), British mystery writer known for her fictional characters Hercule Poirot and Miss Marple.

Colette (1873–1954), pen name of French novelist Sidonie-Gabrielle Colette, who turned to fiction after a career as music-hall dancer.

Noel Coward (1873–1954), English playwright and composer of popular music.

Jamie Lee Curtis (b. 1958), American film actress and daughter of actors Tony Curtis and Janet Leigh.

Tom DeLay (b. 1947), conservative Republican from Texas and former U.S. House majority leader.

Bob Edwards (b. 1947), American journalist and broadcast commentator.

Paul Ehrlich (b. 1932), entomologist who turned to study of human overpopulation; best known for 1968 book *The Population Bomb*.

Katherine Ellison (b. 1957), Pulitzer Prize–winning investigative journalist and author of *The Mommy Brain*.

Ralph Waldo Emerson (1803–1882), American poet, essayist, philosopher, and founder of the Transcendentalist movement.

Nora Ephron (b. 1941), screenwriter, director, novelist, and columnist.

Louise Erdrich (b. 1954), author of novels, poetry, and children's books and enrolled member of the Anishinaabe nation of Native Americans.

Suzanne Farrell (b. 1945), principal ballerina with New York City Ballet known for her work with famed choreographer George Balanchine.

James George Frazer (1854–1941), Scottish anthropologist, author of *The Golden Bough*.

Betty Friedan (1921–2006), feminist activist and writer.

Erich Fromm (1900–1980), psychologist and author.

Carlos Fuentes (b. 1928), Mexican novelist and commentator on politics and popular culture.

Frank Gehry (b. 1929), groundbreaking postmodernist architect.

Charlotte Perkins Gilman (1860–1935), American writer and social reformer.

Ruth Bader Ginsburg (b. 1933), associate justice of the U.S. Supreme Court.

Whoopi Goldberg (b. 1955), actress and comedian.

Ellen Goodman (b. 1941), Pulitzer Prize–winning essayist.

Elaine Heffner (b. 1926), therapist and author of *Mothering: the emotional experience of motherhood after Freud and feminism.*

Arianna Huffington (b. 1950), author and syndicated columnist known for renouncing former conservatism in favor of an embrace of populism.

Zora Neale Hurston (1891–1960), novelist and essayist, known as one of the leading figures of the Harlem Renaissance.

Erica Jong (b. 1942), novelist and poet, best known for feminist novel *Fear of Flying.*

Rose Kennedy (1890–1995), Kennedy family matriarch, mother of nine children including U.S. president John Fitzgerald Kennedy.

Jean Kerr (1922–2003), American author and playwright best known for her humorous take on suburban life, *Please Don't Eat the Daisies.*

Jeane J. Kirkpatrick (1926–2006), ambassador to the United Nations.

Ann Landers (1918–2002), syndicated advice columnist.

Fran Lebowitz (b. 1950), essayist known for sharp-tongued observations and social commentary on American life and popular culture

Gypsy Rose Lee (1911/1914–1970), actress and burlesque performer whose relationship with her mother inspired the stage musical and film *Gypsy*.

Richard Lewis (b. 1947), American comedian and actor.

Madonna (b. 1958), pop singer, actress, and children's rights activist born Madonna Louise Ciccone.

David Mamet (b. 1947), American playwright, screenwriter, film director, and author.

Judith Martin (b. 1938), etiquette columnist known as "Miss Manners."

Phyllis McGinley (1905–1978), author of children's books and poet of suburban life.

David O. McKay (1873–1970), ninth president of the Church of Latter-Day Saints.

Margaret Mead (1901–1978), cultural anthropologist best known for her studies of gender, marital, and sexual practices.

Golda Meir (1898–1978), one of the founders of the state of Israel and its fourth prime minister.

 Mum Is *Always* Right

Toni Morrison (b. 1931), Nobel- and Pulitzer Prize–winning author who examines the contemporary African American experience in America.

Sandra Day O'Connor (b. 1930), first woman to serve as associate justice of the U.S. Supreme Court.

Jacqueline Kennedy Onassis (1929–1994), former first lady.

Dorothy Parker (1893–1967), critic and writer of fiction and verse known for sardonic wit; member of the Algonquin Round Table.

Nancy Pelosi (b. 1940), California representative to Congress and first female Speaker of the House of Representatives.

Sally Rand (1904–1979), actress and dancer known for the fan dance.

Joan Rivers (b. 1933), comic and television personality.

Cokie Roberts (b. 1943), American journalist, author, and radio and television commentator.

Betty Rollin (b. 1936), author and former news correspondent.

Ann Romney (b. 1949), wife of U.S. politician Mitt Romney.

Rita Rudner (b. 1956), U.S. comedian and writer.

Wilma Rudolph (1940–1994), track and field athlete who won three gold medals in the 1960 Olympics.

Joan Benoit Samuelson (b. 1957), American track athlete, first gold medalist in the women's marathon in the Olympics.

Margaret Sanger (1879–1966), American birth control activist.

Patricia Schroeder (b. 1940), former member of the U.S. House of Representatives.

Florida Scott-Maxwell (1883–1979), memoirist known for celebration of aging in *The Measure of My Days*.

Jane Smiley (b. 1949), U.S. novelist and winner of the Pulitzer Prize.

Benjamin Spock, (1903–1998), pediatrician famed for his book *Baby and Child Care*.

Gloria Steinem (b. 1934), feminist activist and author and founder of *Ms.* magazine.

Meryl Streep (b. 1949), Academy Award–winning American actress.

Ann Taylor (1782–1866), British author of verse for children.

Twyla Tharp (b. 1941), American dancer and choreographer whose work has been honored with both Tony and Emmy awards.

Margaret Thatcher (b. 1925), first woman to serve as British prime minister.

Usher (b. 1978), professional name of Usher Raymond, R&B and pop singer, record producer, and part owner of Cleveland Cavaliers basketball team.

Abigail Van Buren (b. 1918), advice columnist known as "Dear Abby."

Kristin van Ogtrop (b. 1964), American magazine editor and essayist.

Elizabeth Vargas (b. 1962), television journalist.

Marilyn vos Savant (b. 1946), American holder of "Highest IQ" record in *Guinness Book of World Records* who writes a weekly column in *Parade* magazine.

John Waters (b. 1946), American filmmaker and writer known for offbeat humor.

Hannah Whitall Smith (1832–1911), American-born social reformer, author, and lay preacher.

Kate Douglas Wiggin (1856–1923), U.S. educator and children's book author.

Lois Wyse (1926–2007), columnist and author of more than sixty books often touching on family life.

Henny Youngman (1926–1998), comic master of the one-liner.

Index

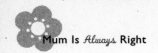

Mum Is *Always* Right

Mum Is *Always* Right

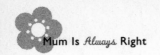
Mum Is *Always* Right